You Always Belonged and You Always Will

You Always Belonged and You Always Will

a Philosophy of Belonging

By Dr. Martin Clay Fowler

Text copyright © 2014 Dr. Martin Clay Fowler
All Rights Reserved
ISBN: 0615931324
ISBN: 978-0-615-93132-6

Dedicated to Beth G. Raps and Laura J. Nigro
This book belongs to you two, and it always will.

TABLE OF CONTENTS

**PART ONE:
WHERE ELSE WOULD LIFE BELONG?** 1

    Chapter 1: 4 Stories and
    a Manifesto About Belonging 3

    Chapter 2: 25 Meditations on Belonging . . 23

    Chapter 3: Animal Crackers 45

    Chapter 4: Please remain seated 69

    Chapter 5: Rethinking Discipline 89

**PART TWO: COURAGE, JUSTICE,
PEACE, TRUTH, AND LOVE** 107

    Chapter 6: Power and Speed
    Belonging with Courage 109

    Chapter 7: Strength and Flexibility The
    Reach of Justice Against Resistance . . .131

TABLE OF CONTENTS

**Chapter 8: Balance and Coordination
Moving in Peace** 151

**Chapter 9: Agility and Accuracy
Truth be Nimble, Truth be Quick** 171

**Chapter 10: Endurance and Stamina
Love's Suffering and Hope** 187

PART THREE: LIVING WITHIN LIVES 205

**Chapter 11: The Politics of
Transformation** 207

Chapter 12: Virtual Belonging 231

Chapter 13: To Boldly Belong 251

Chapter 14: 25 Epigrams 271

Bibliography. 279

Endnotes 283

Preface

J. Steven Griffin took the black and white photograph of me on the cover of this book (and the one on the last page) almost forty years ago. I chose these photos not for sentimental value but because they convey how I feel about belonging. That's very hard to put into words, yet when I look at the photos, the warmth and assurance of the book's title "You always belonged and you always will" come through. I hope that it does for you, and that you have some photo or memory of your own with that special quality.

In different ways, I've worked on belonging for a long time, not because I crave to belong, but because the phenomenon of belonging is a puzzle. For years, I organized a monthly potluck for gay and lesbian scientists, providing food and fellowship for people who were otherwise strangers. I've volunteered with the St. Philip's Jail Ministry, visiting and praying with inmates in the Durham County Jail on Saturday mornings. For both groups, I wanted to show and ensure that people do belong even when they're marginalized or isolated from others.

I began teaching a course about restorative justice. I taught another course called "Animal Captivity" in which students debated how captive animals are members of our community, and even whether animals should be captive at all. When I taught the philosophy of space exploration and environmental stewardship, human belonging could not be taken for granted. Can people rightly belong within Earth's life? Can humans ever truly belong on other worlds?

For many years, I was a leader in *Evangelicals Concerned Western Region* – long before anyone took same-sex marriage seriously. And being an evangelical Christian in a same-sex marriage has been a rocky 30-year story about belonging.

You don't have to strain to see this theme of belonging at work. Yet each time it showed up, I was quite taken by surprise. Like the tombstone epitaph: *"This is the last place I expected to be,"* my exploration of and advocacy for belonging put me in new places. I had no advance itinerary mapped out to understand where to find belonging, but I still wound up where I belonged. I think that's how transformation works. I think that belonging is essentially *vulnerability to some transformation with a destination that's unexpected but also exactly what should have been expected.*

I'm dedicating this book in deep gratitude to Beth G. Raps and Laura Nigro who have worked with me and encouraged me through several versions of the text. My colleagues in the Philosophy Department of Elon University have likewise belonged with me in my teaching for the past twenty years and that has meant a great deal to me.

I want most to acknowledge you as a person who cares about belonging. You agree that the topic matters. Perhaps you wonder how belonging is even possible in a world which makes it so difficult. The need to belong is fundamental to being human. We ask: *Can we belong? Should we belong? Why are so many unable to belong? Who deserves to belong? How can we learn to belong*? Philosophy has considered many questions about the human condition, but has said little about belonging, perhaps because philosophers have such a vocational stake in remaining detached. Why should philosophers – and the rest of us – take belonging seriously now?

Now is the time because nature's cry to humans is mounting: *"Act as though you belong here!"* Not knowing (or caring) about how to belong and presuming

Preface

to judge any life as not belonging creates gratuitous distress and needless violence. So, I wrote this book – not as the last word about belonging, but to encourage others to think, talk, write, and find ways of practice that honor and advocate for belonging, for humans and nonhumans alike.

The first job is to acknowledge that, although many do not feel much belonging, belonging is already a done deal. Emotionally, that's a very hard sell, and this is where philosophy is needed. The second and harder job is to *think, feel, and act* as though belonging is a done deal. The good news is that working out the terms of belonging is doable. It makes more sense than believing the lie that belonging is scarce: a prize for the lucky, the deserving, and the few.

If you want to dialogue about belonging and transformation, please write to me at martin@zuberfowler.com. I look forward to hearing from you.

PART ONE

WHERE ELSE WOULD LIFE BELONG?

CHAPTER 1
4 Stories and a Manifesto About Belonging

In his *Meditations,* Descartes tried to show that "I think, therefore I am" proves the existence of God and the external world. I'm equally ambitious, but I have a different goal. I want to convince you that *you belong, therefore you matter.* In Chapter 2, I develop this idea in 25 meditations of my own. For now, though, I invite you to read four short stories from my life which taught me plenty about belonging in situations where belonging was hard to find.

The first story is about a silent confrontation in front of a church. Churches are very belonging-mindful institutions. The second story describes my yearlong PTSD recovery "from the inside out" after being crushed in an auto collision. After being vulnerable to serious trauma, I recovered by learning vulnerability to transformation. The third story is about visiting people in the Durham County Jail every Saturday with the St. Philip's jail ministry. Volunteers act as though "You belong, therefore you matter" is the way things are despite walls and locks which banish people to places of non-belonging. The last very short story is included for fun. Just how do you belong when you get fired?

These four stories are followed by a manifesto. This manifesto is my bold "this I believe" proclamation to inspire you to claim your belonging. If you'll allow me to stand on a soapbox to address you in this way, I promise that you'll take away a new perspective on "you belong."

Church on the Curb. Here is my first story. Twenty-seven years ago, my husband and I hunted a church to join in our small Texas town. The church had handed us a leaflet entitled "Belong Where You Live" which featured footprints leading to a church and made the claim that joining a local congregation made believers more effective Christians. But the pastor and deacon were quite unnerved by us sitting in their pews. They tried to return our collection plate offering and begged us to get out. In response, we sat on the curb across from the front of the church where we read the Bible each Sunday morning.

The congregation began entering the church's back door to avoid seeing us. Some wanted to welcome us, and the rest wanted to ignore us or chase us away. They thought we belonged someplace else. More accurately, they deemed that we did not belong. We neither went into the church nor left during that spring. We simply parked our butts on the curb and read the Bible. We lived in the neighborhood, and we belonged where we lived. Teenagers understand hanging out as belonging where they live when they've got no adult-sanctioned place to belong. Our church on the curb expressed our spiritual intuition that we belonged. It was not a ploy to pry open the church to admit gay people. They never welcomed us. We never alerted the media because this was no protest. It was a spiritual exercise but not a vigil. We didn't hold candles to symbolize our solemn awareness of a cause greater than ourselves. We weren't pouting or waiting to be invited inside. We just belonged in the sense of being openly vulnerable to whatever transformation God had in store.

Belonging is presence more than loitering, but not any less than that either. We hung out in the neighborhood where we lived, just as the church's "Belong Where You Live" booklet instructed. Would the church's belonging problem vanish had we scooted down the street out of sight? I don't think so. We saw dramatic confirmation that, when people declare that others don't belong, their own sense of belonging becomes inexplicably unhinged and jeopardized. Theologically, we believed that Christians belong to one and the same body of believers, and that it's spiritually wrong to pretend otherwise. So, we didn't behave otherwise. We belonged bearing witness.

You might not be convinced that God actually told us "you belong," but we were convinced that we'd received that blessing. That made all the difference. Though we didn't therefore feel that we mattered much, we suddenly mattered a great deal to that church. Had we not belonged, had we not received that blessing, why would that church care so much about us? If all the belonging was guarded inside that church, why did they feel hoisted into the air on the wrong end of a seesaw by two guys worshipping quietly across the street?

Suffering as a Seed of Belonging. Here is my second story. One rainy night on the highway, nine years ago, a drunk driver plowed his SUV into the back of my tiny red Honda Civic,  crushing it like a beer can. Paramedics pried open the car so that a helicopter could fly me to the hospital. Amazingly, I had no broken bones and recovered from concussion and hematomas with no memory of the collision. My rattled brain's yearlong PTSD journey began. I felt as though I belonged nowhere, even in long-familiar places. "Here" and "there" no longer felt anything like *my* "here and there." Love and reassurance helped and communicated unmistakably and preciously "You belong." But jagged parts of my personality no longer belonged together as pieces of the old self-puzzle.

If those pieces were ever going to fit together, it would be on new terms to make a new picture. I could drive, work, talk, and function, but had little sense of place, inside or out. During trauma recovery, different aspects of the self slowly rediscovered each other and found new togetherness as a self capable of transformation into ...what? I couldn't be restored to who I was prior to the collision. I could not resign myself to remain in this purgatory of non-belonging. I had no confidence that I would find any "new normal" with my GPS. Instead, I chose to be open to belonging on new terms. We don't usually think of vulnerability as something fierce, but I knew that opening my mind and body in diverse and ferocious ways was how I would find belonging.[1]

It's important to place this story in perspective. There are thousands of such collisions in our society every year, though we act as though they are infrequent and belong nowhere in driving as usual. That's the dubious part of what we mean by "accident." I guess we have to believe that lie in order to put ourselves behind the wheel day after day. Also, damaged brains matter much more than broken bones, but we are quicker to sympathize with crutches than with the unseen hurting brain. We make a place for broken bones in everyday life, but not for broken minds. That said, whether the trauma happens on the highway or in a war zone, PTSD is not just recovery of function and meaning, but becoming newly changed into an intact self who belongs on new terms.

We usually take our intact selves for granted and puzzle over how that self fits into the world or can change the world to its liking. But cranial trauma yanks away that assumption. The fractured self can't belong as it did, as it wishes to, as it needs to do. From the inside out, recovery is like a salmon swimming furiously and ceaselessly upstream even when the journey is exhausting and believing in a destination feels silly. From the outside, this looks like blind denial. I don't understand how the splintered self-shards "know" that they belong in relationship with each other and their world. How do they know it with enough conviction to sustain hope for months to risk transformation? However, being reminded by love and kindness, and challenging oneself when the challenges feel burdensome, means risking vulnerability in the slim but sturdy hope of becoming. That's transformation just across the horizon.

You may have found out the hard way about trauma recovery as a belonging pilgrimage. Maybe you're still on such a trek. You may not have reached any shrine or closure. Or maybe you need encouragement to hope that belonging awaits and is worth the journey. Keep striving, but life is not just about striving. It's greatest gift – first to the living and then to the cosmos – is belonging. So, bet that this gift is there for you. Don't be disappointed when it doesn't look or feel as you expected. If it's different, then maybe you are too. That's what transformation means.

Sometimes communities and nations go through belonging traumas, scarred by war, oppression, atrocity, and genocide. In the aftermath, they don't know what to do with themselves. The world tries to belong with traumatized societies by either giving humanitarian aid or else imposing quarantine and sanctions. In the aftermath of collective suffering, survivors' capacity for transformation seems a very cramped crawl space between atrocity and uncertainty.

But, within that crawl space, they might get more than a change in leadership. There might be political transformation. Sustained fragile vulnerability allows collective traumas to heal. Otherwise, a collective PTSD gets recycled and acted out in feuds, persecutions, and other ways. Politics helps things to become more like they're "supposed to be" when politics finds ways for people to remind each other once more that they belong and therefore matter.

Go Directly to Jail. This is my third story. Twelve years ago, I met a retired college teacher in North Carolina who believed that jail inmates two blocks from our church were *de facto* neighbors of our church, and that we should care for our neighbors. I went with him to visit, and I have felt that I belong there each Saturday morning since. In one sense, courts enforce society's judgment that offenders belong  in jail. In another sense, jails are designed to keep inmates from feeling belonging. This is a photo of me seated between Warren Pope and Richard Watson outside the Durham County Jail. Those two men taught me a great deal about being a neighbor in a very inhospitable facility.

I live in Durham County, North Carolina. My conviction that everyone belongs and therefore matters sends me to visit and pray with inmates in the Durham County Jail on Saturday mornings. Inmates can choose to visit with our volunteers from 9:00 am – 10:00 a.m. With each inmate, I talk and pray through Plexiglas. Inmates have little communication with the outside, so I help them communicate with loved ones by enabling them to choose and send greeting cards.

The presence of our volunteers signifies that inmates still belong in fellowship with believers.

The cards signify that they still have family they care about. I tell them that, with their permission, I will call out their names during our "prayers of the people" on Sunday, so that parishioners can pray for them. I ask those inmates to pray for our church at the same time. That signifies mutual participation in spiritual transformation. None of this raises money for bail or releases any captives. What it does do is remind them that when they feel least remembered by others and least in control of their lives, they nevertheless belong.

In this situation, you learn something remarkable about belonging: *You belong in every other life.* I don't mean that you force your way into lives or spy on people. In fact this isn't about relationships between people. It's about lives belonging within lives. You discover that lives aren't really enclosed by borders. Of course, we act that way, but these encounters point to a different truth. You also learn that every life somehow belongs in yours. That doesn't make your life crowded or exceed maximum capacity. It means that even when you shut people out or treat them like they don't exist, they still belong in your life. My story about the church on the curb is a good example of that. It's not that we're stuck with each other. We're inside each other's lives. This may strike you as weird or mystical, but I think of it as sensible. Where else would life belong?

I would define belonging as vulnerability to transformation. The loss of belonging which inmates feel isn't really about separation and isolation. Many inmates, young and old, are convinced that they won't change, that their life prospects won't improve, or they just don't see how real transformation for them is possible. That's what it means to feel as though you belong nowhere, no matter where you happen to be. When they meet the volunteer who asks "How can I be of service?," a readiness and capacity for transformation can be rekindled in very simple ways. If you find yourself someplace where you're not sure that you belong, you may need some rekindling.

Still not convinced that you belong? I walked into work one Monday morning and was told by the office manager that my boss had fired me for taking too long a vacation. That was a nasty surprise. What would you do? You're probably thinking: *"You're fired, so you don't belong there anymore!"* But I'm someone who believes that everyone belongs, so I wasn't satisfied. I silently sat down at my desk and started working. The flummoxed office manager shouted that I didn't belong there anymore and asked what the hell I thought I was doing. Apparently, I had not comprehended the invincible power of "you're fired!" to banish my puny belonging, especially coming from someone authorized to proclaim it. I replied that I would discuss that with my employer. I kept working.

I quietly feared that she would call the police to throw me out. Instead, she quickly phoned my boss who asked "Doesn't he understand? What does he want?" She conveyed the questions to me. I replied: "I am working. And I want more money." I got a raise.

The real story was that we all tacitly agreed that I really belonged where I worked. The boss could not rescind his decision without losing face. So, if I began with us all belonging (notwithstanding my long vacation and being fired), I could negotiate terms. It sounds crazy, but "you belong, therefore you matter" can mean a raise. Stay ready for real change.

The four stories illustrate the power of "you belong" as the first step in our ethos of transformation. Even when you're kicked out, locked up, crushed, or get fired, you belong, and you always did. Even when it looks crazy to belong where no sane person could hope to belong, you belong, and you always will. That's not wishful thinking. It's simply how we choose to begin. How do I know that you belong? My knowledge is not the point. This is a blessing. And on what authority do I bless you? I'm alive and so are you. This is the first gift of the living to the living.

Regardless of your circumstances and history, no matter whatever else you want, no matter how you suffer, at the heart of your suffering is the promise of belonging: your capacity to become transformed. Maybe you haven't been kicked out of a church, so think of some group that rejected you and how much this hurt and made you angry. Traumas aren't restricted to auto collisions. Think of divorce, unemployment, or cancer. Yes, you strive to survive hard times, but while you suffer, you also yearn to be reminded that you still belong. Then you can figure out how this trauma belongs in the unfolding story of your life.

A Manifesto of Belonging

Another way to convey the power of belonging is to make a manifesto, preferably one that's inspiring and not preachy, provocative rather than dogmatic. This allows us to dwell with belonging by doing bold justice to "you belong" and "you belong, therefore you matter."

**

Without striving, life would not be possible. Without belonging, life would not matter.

4 Stories and a Manifesto About Belonging

You've always felt, long before you had words for it, *that every life belongs in this world.* Not in the next world, not in some better world, but in this world. Yet you haven't dared to believe what you've felt until now. Without exception, kudzu and mosquitoes belong. All living things, locked away or running free, thriving or endangered, belong. During the Earth's *Great Dying* 252.28 million years ago (the Permian-Triassic extinction), 96% of all marine life, 70% of all land vertebrates, and every single insect perished. Notwithstanding this calamity, they all belonged.

Together, they densely populated and transformed the matrix of life and life's history on Earth across millions of years. Belonging is not tenure, not a success story, not a popularity contest. Belonging is not inner at-oneness or special membership. Belonging is the royal *via transformativa* paved with your unadorned vulnerabilities to those qualitative changes which we call transformation. You might hide them as weaknesses, but, across eons, you call life's vulnerability *evolution.* Across your life, you call it by many names: maturity, intimacy, teachability, completion, or being reborn.

Go ahead and doubt that anything in this precarious life is certain, *except that you and every other life belong.* Let that be your axiom. Each life belongs in every life, and every life belongs in each life. Don't wait for proof, permission, better arrangements or new management. This is your unconditional, non-contingent, and non-negotiable gift. Don't fret that humanity has lost belonging in this world. Who the hell are you to judge whether any life belongs? Let the sheer rightness and inescapable blessedness of belonging on Earth ring true for you, instead of waiting in vain for invitation, permission, redemption, membership, affiliation, inclusion or some other reason to finally belong.

You despair that humans are unworthy to belong because they show up everywhere, but belong nowhere in nature. Humans often behave as though they don't belong, but destructive life: locusts, termites, and bumbling people, still belong. There is no "non-belonging" zone for life. Humans have made life hard or impossible for many species, but the very fact that humans belong makes them most accountable for that hardship. Belonging isn't a special treat deserved only by the blameless. It's a stupendous broad bequest by the living to the living. You can't pay it back. Remember the countless ways, great and small, that life made it miraculously possible for you to fully accept my benediction: "*You belong.*" Give thanks for the unexpectedly profound and casually banal fact that you belong on Earth just like every other life, and as part of every life! Packed in your "some" are incredible kinds of belonging! What glorious healing ways of belonging you might provide! How silly to pretend that people don't belong, never did, and never will.

Don't blame philosophers for your skepticism about people belonging. Yes, they love detachment, and their vocational liability has given us new ways of belonging with our doubts and questions. However, philosophers don't think much about belonging. It's no Platonic star in the constellation of truth, beauty, goodness and justice. Nor does belonging provoke philosophical questions about knowledge, right and wrong, or the meaning of life (yet). Thinkers enamored with "a place for everything and everything in its place," might obsess about belonging as bean counting and sorting, but that's about it. Of course they want to belong as much as you do, whether to their quest or someplace where they can quest in peace; Socrates, stubbornly belonged to an ungrateful Athens unto death, and submitted to execution with only as much certainty about his soul's transformations as his dialectic could provide.

Don't blame Aristotle. Yes, belonging within his schema of genus and species isn't all you might hope for. In those Hollywood Squares, Aristotle's box of *rational animal* isn't much of a home, and besides, evolution has liens on it. However, in ethics and politics, Aristotle knew that it takes belonging in a polis to make a citizen. When the polis turns against you, escape to Macedonia. For all their detached rationalism, Descartes and Spinoza hunted persecution-free places to belong in Europe. So let's not blame philosophers. Somehow you wound up believing that people do not belong in this world. Yet don't you find it exasperating and dispiriting to live with people (you included) who believe that they don't belong? In our skepticism, we hardly know how to face each other and belong together anew. Even when you're wired together with others as tightly as a prairie dog colony, each ducks into his or her own burrow for security.

Ask what our world could be like if everyone belonged? Ask instead: What could the world be like when people redirect life to quests other than belonging? They'd stop pretending that people don't belong. We would collaborate with inmates, refugees, illegals, homeless, wild animals, and every other class of non-belongers to effectively honor their belonging.

Live as you choose, or live as you must, but belong while you live.

Do you still clutch belonging in a proprietary way, like money, rights, skin, mate, or territory, as though these personal possessions or "belongings" are enough? Unless you first belong, with all the hope and fragility of this vulnerability, you've got nowhere to enjoy your belongings. Whether you sit in a penthouse or crouch on the curb like a bag lady, the only vulnerability you're likely to feel is fear of losing your stuff or having no secure place for it. Unless your life belongs in every life, and each life belongs in yours, you belong nowhere and you'll never be confident that, of course, you do belong.

Belonging does not cast a long shadow. *Belonging is that long shadow which your life casts!* It goes with you everywhere and reminds you that you have substance and a changing relationship with light. Its size and shape reveals how you're stretched, squeezed, or standing underneath transformation. Like your shadow, belonging reveals your life's place and direction. In Plato's allegory of the cave,[2] the reader wonders whether the chained prisoners looking at shadows belong in their captivity or above ground with the escapee in sunny enlightenment. But those shadows are the perfect allegory for belonging. Unenlightened, the prisoners stare at shadows not comprehending that what they see are shadows. Likewise, we belong without knowing that we belong. The prisoners think of what they see on the cave wall as enduring external realities, just as we imagine true belonging as "out there" in someone's control and utterly removed from ourselves. Plato neglects to mention that the sunlit escapee now casts a shadow. He belongs. Now he must figure out where and how to honor that belonging.

And so must you. My manifesto is over, so I'll step down from the soapbox. Don't feel pressured to belong. I can't make you belong. I won't even try. In fact, you can't even make yourself belong. Don't waste your breath. But if the belonging you feel among and for the living is something you can believe, and believing it with gratitude, you want to guide your actions accordingly, your small life will cast a very long shadow. How are you willing, able, and ready for your life to be transformed? How can you give others firm confidence to believe that they belong, and not lose hope? When you despair that nothing really changes, you know perfectly well that change is everywhere. What you mean is that nothing and no one is *transformed*. "You belong" changes that.

Welcome home.

CHAPTER 2
25 Meditations on Belonging

1. *You belong.* You always did, and you always will. How do I know? These two words are not about my knowledge. "You belong" is my benediction to you, not some claim about you. On what authority do I extend this blessing to you? I am alive, and belonging is the first and most important gift of the living to the living. So, anyone alive can extend this blessing to you, including your dog. Whether you accept this gift is up to you. You probably have plenty of questions peppered with prepositions and indirect objects: Belong to whom? Belong with what? Belong here? Belong now? Belong just how exactly? Yet you know intuitively that this is a real gift and a good one. It's a blessing

you needed even if you never considered asking for it. Extend it to me and I'm grateful for it too without being able to explain why.

2. *You belong* could be a reciprocal exchange between two strangers, two opponents, two lovers, or between the powerful and the less powerful. It is not a superficial social courtesy such as "Have a nice day." It's not my benign affirmation that you're okay and I'm okay. Nor am I claiming that you belong. I'm giving words which, in my giving, give form to the truth that you belong. The blessing you receive invokes your belonging, not as word magic but as our word commitment. It's not that I make your belonging appear out of nowhere. My two words (which are now yours) mean that your belonging was never "nowhere" in the first place. You belong. You always did and you always will. That said, let's get on with life.

3. Suppose that we start encountering each other with this blessing, spoken or silent: new possibilities appear and certain threats are banished. Are we inexplicably more respectful and hospitable and less likely to hurt each other? I think so, and we don't need ethics (yet) to make it so. It's easier to bless those we like or identify with, but we'll discover that

this benediction is pretty rugged for inhospitable places. For now, let's start where we can and see what follows. It's an unfamiliar way to begin an encounter – or a philosophy – yet it rings true.

4. It's new because, when I share this blessing, your belonging is no longer something problematic and probationary. Your belonging is no tentative perk which I might grant or revoke. Your belonging is not a distant romanticized sweet place you can only yearn for. *It's the way things are,* because we are both alive and I share this blessing with you. We may then welcome or exclude each other. You can accept, refuse, or negotiate the terms. Maybe you're lost. But you belong, notwithstanding. Your belonging isn't something I have the power to make or unmake. Power has more humane uses.

5. These 25 Meditations begin with my blessing, even if this strikes you as presumptuous wishful thinking. You are pretty sure that you have issues with belonging. They may be emotional, social, political, or starkly existential. Somehow, you don't fit in or you just don't know what to do with yourself. Besides, who could ever belong in such a world? And how

could I know anything about those problems of yours? Still, I invite you to begin this journey with me at this spot where you hear me say *"You Belong."* It is an ironic first step because this step doesn't really belong anywhere (yet) in our cultural and intellectual landscape.

Happily, you don't need to make a paradigm shift or revolutionize your thinking. You don't need to learn new jargon or slay oppressive systems. The blessing simply but powerfully directs you to an unfamiliar point of departure: *You belong.* This is not belonging as a given but belonging as a *giving.* It sounds odd if you think of belonging as your status, accomplishment, or turf. Belonging's what you need or defend. Take your belonging off the table, and what do you have to talk about with me? Plenty, I'll bet.

6. René Descartes is famous for his declaration in the *Meditations*: "I think, therefore I am." Descartes commended this claim as "clear and distinct," meaning beyond doubt, but it's been criticized over the centuries as a dubious inference and a bad point of departure for epistemology. With these cautions in mind, what can we infer from "You belong?" *"You belong, therefore you matter."* After all, try to prove that you matter, and you eventually appeal to some belonging; to God, with significant others, to

your unique mortal existence, in some dear place, or within a privileged cultural niche which (hopefully) never questions whether you matter. Not to your face, anyway.

But it follows from my benediction "You belong" that you do matter. "You matter" is packed (but not hidden) inside "You belong," waiting to be released. That's not because we define belonging as mattering. We'll get to the definition below. "Therefore" does not reveal something true by definition. Nor is "therefore" a logical linchpin between two independent claims. It joins a benediction to a claim. "Therefore" traces that path of understanding which you follow upon hearing that you belong. You receive that gift and therefore know that you matter.

7. We still need a definition for belonging. When I say "You belong," I speak as someone who's alive to you as a living person who's not merely subject to quantitative change like a rock or a physical system but also vulnerable to qualitative change or *transformation*. I suggest that life's belonging – including yours - can be defined as *vulnerability to transformation*. The vulnerability may be intentional or unintentional, chosen or not.

Take time to reflect on this definition because it may not be anything like what you usually mean by "belonging." *Belonging is vulnerability to transformation.* Do you want to belong? Very well, what kind of vulnerability can you bring? What sort of qualitative change are you ready for? Before you judge your vulnerability as weakness, consider that it might be part of your belonging. Before you worry that some vulnerability will undermine your belonging, consider that it might unfold new belonging. If you were as invulnerable to transformation as Superman or ageless as Peter Pan, you would also have as many belonging issues as Superman and Peter Pan.

8. Now that we have a working though unfamiliar definition, do you still need my benediction? Why can't you dispense with me and speak in the first person like Descartes, proclaiming: *"I belong"* and *"I belong, therefore I matter?"* Because you've already learned the hard way that it doesn't work. Remember the times you've tried to do just that? Puberty is full of these desperate first person strivings. Each try leads to dead ends, convolutions, and feeling like the wrong spare part. That's what happens when you try to "make" yourself belong. "I belong" is whistling the wrong tune in the dark. First, belonging isn't something you discover through introspection or by observation. Nor do you make belonging so by your resolve and fiat.

Second, belonging isn't a striving. Striving is transforming your internal or external environment. Belonging means being *transformed by your environment*. "Transformation" is not a fancy word for change. We call it "*real* change," but it's quite different from change. Instead of changing a status quo, transformation replaces it, not as abrupt revolution, but as substantial alteration.

You can describe the size and duration of a change. You can judge a change. But a transformation is transition which has a "rightness" about it that trumps judgment. For example, when I say that you're "transformed," I don't mean improved, or reformed. I mean that you are a new person. Transformation can feel momentous, but, if you're ready and the time is right, it can happen as casually as turning a corner. Likewise, if you want to make an impact in the world, you don't just want change. Any rock can make an impact. You want to make a difference, and that's ordinary everyday transformation.

Positive changes may feel good, but, weirdly, transformation feels positive even when you can't yet show that it's any good. When you're on the receiving end of transformation, you can't identify or measure it like a change. That's the situation for belonging, so we invariably rely upon, and place authority in, someone else (virtually anyone, really) to confirm our belonging. In fact, you'd hardly ever say "I belong" aloud unless you were clarifying your membership or protesting your exclusion. That's why "I belong" rings hollow, and "I belong, therefore I matter" scarcely rings at all. What you say is true, but you're not the one to say it.

9. *"You belong, therefore you matter"* is not one claim entailed by another. It is one claim disclosed and revealed by a benediction. My blessing "You belong" does not logically compel the truth that you matter. Just as belonging turns time and space into story and place, my two words remind you descriptively, emotionally, spiritually, and socially not just that you're alive, but that you're alive, *and rightly so.* My blessing does not bestow your belonging. You don't even need a human being to do the blessing. As the primary gift of living to the living, you may experience this blessing extended to you without words by nature, if you're open to receive it. In the woods, you may feel with intuitive and emotional certainty that you belong, and therefore you matter. On the other hand, if you find yourself lost in the woods, remember to leave room to receive this blessing from the plants and animals around you: *you belong, you*

always did, and you always will. Then worry about finding your compass and directions.

10. Since we began with Descartes, who prized certainty of axioms and method, consider why it is it so hard for you to know without a doubt that you belong. Your belonging is not a self-evident truth. Sadly, this truth may be disputed, denied, and trampled on a daily basis. You can look deep within, look far without, and your belonging's nowhere to be found. And yet, you do belong. Count your vulnerabilities, or your blessings if you prefer, but they don't add up to belonging. Focus on a promising slice of life - your most emotionally attached and intimate relationships in which you most feel belonging - and your belonging shrinks to an oasis in a vast desert. What will you do for belonging in the rest of your life when you leave the oasis?

11. If you've felt alone in a crowd or suffocated by a dysfunctional relationship, then you're not counting on prolonged proximity for belonging. Being sure that you belong is tough because, if belonging is about your vulnerability to transformation, this kind of vulnerability is lodged in your blind spot. It's like a proprioceptive "feel" that you're situated in

such-and-such a way even though you can't see that it's so. The good news is that you can know that you belong without being able to point to "your belonging."

The bad news is that, if you come to doubt your belonging for any reason, then the combined resources of your reason, reflection, immersion, and self-reassurance are inadequate to answer nagging doubts about whether you belong. Not one single thing, however meaningful, proves that you belong. Your belonging is a great truth about your life that you are perversely (or perhaps wisely) ill-equipped to appreciate and confirm by yourself. In a culture where your belonging is treated as probationary, provisional, privileged or impossible, knowing with any certainty that you belong is even harder. Therefore, the blessing "You belong" is subversively and profoundly interpersonal without being especially social. It's receiving the gift of belonging, after all, that turns isolation into blessed solitude.

12. Does "You belong" already presuppose that you matter? Is the value of your life a rabbit hidden inside the belonging hat? I don't think so. Belonging considered as vulnerability to transformation is no tautology which says the same thing twice only in different words. Whether you belong, fit in, know what to do

with yourself, and wind up exactly where you should be or are meant to be, none of this presumes that your life amounts to a hill of beans - even if the beans are wonderfully as they should be. Compare "You belong, therefore you matter" with "I love you, therefore you matter," "You are a good person, therefore you matter," or "You are the best, therefore you matter." These inferences make your life's value contingent upon something else being true. However, "You belong, therefore you matter" does not. The value of your life is manifest in your belonging, not hostage to it.

13. And this is a powerful place to begin. "*You belong*" preveniently disempowers all the abuse otherwise permitted by the judgment that you *don't* belong or the lingering accusation that you might not belong. "You belong" won't topple systems of bias, discrimination, and probationary exclusion like so many card houses, but the real estate value of those houses will drop considerably. It's now a buyer's market. If you already belong, the stakes for acceptance and rejection are not so high.

Likewise, well-intentioned initiatives to expand the circle, be inclusive, and embody radical welcome (variations on belonging as a communal striving) now look like disaster-relief repair crews dispatched to the wrong places. There's nothing to repair. You already belong; you always did and you always will. So, how can we treat each other so as to honor that belonging? Blest as belonging, you're liberated from a limbo in which too many of us languish. You are free to be yourself anew and with others with new confidence, conviction, hospitality, and gratitude.

14. This is the most basic and important spiritual blessing that a person can extend to life, and it is more fundamental than the blessings of any one religious tradition. Are you ready to share this blessing? From whom would you withhold it? To whom would you give it freely? It does not solve all the problems of religious pluralism, but "you belong" has much to recommend it as a reciprocal point of departure. What makes it sincere and not just empty words? *Gratitude.*

The speaker is grateful for life which belongs. That's how it feels to give the blessing, and that's how it feels to receive (and not simply hear) the blessing. But the blessing does not itemize appreciation for this and that. It's thanks for your life – not approval - because *"You belong, therefore you matter"* is not contingent upon your life satisfying a moral standard or my personal bar of acceptance. It's deeply normative but says more about your life's substance than does any particular norm. This is not confirmation that you lead a worthwhile life. The invocation upholds that your life matters enough to live in worthwhile ways. That may seem cold comfort and consolation if your sense of belonging is tenuous, but it can also be an important reminder.

15. If we admire this blessing so much that we recommend it for everyone, is it suitable for framing as a binding duty? In the spirit of Immanuel Kant, you could rework my blessing into a categorical imperative. Instead of declaring like Kant "Act only according to that maxim whereby you can, at the same time, will that it should become a universal law," you declare "*Act as though you and every other person (or life) belongs.*" But this generous moral commandment makes it easy to forget that you first took the time to bless, and you did not bless because of a maxim. I think that belonging does involve distinctive rights and duties, but we shouldn't jump to maxims and duties too quickly.

16. You may wonder how you could belong even though you may not feel that way. Think of your

belonging as vulnerability to transformation. That's not feeling vulnerable or experiencing transformation. It's the emotional equivalent of the Boy Scout motto: "Be prepared." You feel ready yet you don't know for what. This reminds me of a scene in the Monty Pythonesque movie *Time Bandits* in which characters try to exploit holes in the fabric of Creation but bump into an unseen obstacle and exclaim: "Oh! So *that's* what an invisible barrier looks like! So, this is what belonging looks like.

This is what transformation looks like! A coach sees this vulnerability (or teachability) in a promising athlete. Also, animals – including you - typically experience this "readiness" to belong while in motion, not when sedentary. It's hard to be transformed by an environment that you don't explore. But you might feel no belonging for a simpler reason: You don't want or intend to be transformed just now. You won't submit to it. Yet you belong despite the fact you don't want to. You belong even though you'd rather not. You belong, even if you're unable or unwilling to experience it. In this respect, your belonging is unconditional and non-negotiable, and maybe you're the one who put up the invisible barrier.

17. If your belonging is not hostage to your desires and goals, that does sound like a Kantian shift

from hypothetical imperatives to a categorical one. Categorical or not, a duty to *act as though every life belongs* can still be good moral hygiene when in the company of people you dislike or don't want to be around. Aren't there people in your life who just don't belong "there?" That's the equivalent of wishing them dead.

If you do not think that death wishes belong in your life, act as though you and everyone you encounter belongs. Moreover, each dismissal by which you regard others as not belonging chips away at your own sense of legitimate belonging. If their belonging is probationary, then there's no reason to exclude yours. Whatever rush you get from banishing another life is followed by lack of confidence in your own belonging.

18. "You belong" is different than declaring "I respect you (as a person)." Respect acknowledges a special status, entitlement, standing and dignity. Respect is what you're entitled to or what we owe each other as persons. However, we don't owe each other belonging. None of us is entitled to belong, none of us owes belonging to each other, and yet we depend on others to bless our belonging. Belonging is a gift.

19. Biological definitions of life typically include processes such as metabolism, adaptation, homeostasis, growth, and reproduction, implicitly assuming that life consists of functional strivings which transform life's internal and external environments. Within this mindset, life of any sort looks very, very busy – ceaselessly so. Apart from mortality, vulnerabilities and weaknesses are not essential to how we define life. But life is also vulnerable to transformation. Otherwise, evolution would be impossible. What if life's story is equally about belonging and striving? Life transforms environments to make life possible. Life is likewise transformed by environments in order to belong. When we shoehorn all life processes into talk of desperate organic strivings, we might miss life's signature success: a changing matrix of belonging. Life doesn't just sustain itself; life enables life to belong.

20. What's true for nature is often true for culture. Each culture decides how striving and belonging relatively matter and normalizes some ratio between transforming and being transformed. That produces culture dynamism as well as dysfunction. A society prioritizing striving will try to increase control and reduce vulnerability. Its members may feel safety,

security, and comfort; they may belong insofar as they participate in the striving, yet otherwise feel devoid of belonging in how they treat each other.

A striving individualist, whether rugged or just ragged, still needs to hear "You belong" and know that "You belong, therefore you matter." On the other hand, if your society favors belonging over striving, you might fear that conformity will discourage new striving. Here it helps to think of belonging not as conformity, but as vulnerability to transformation. You and/or your group can valorize such risky belonging rather than conformity. Otherwise, you and everyone in your community will feel more or less trapped.

21. What's the sweetest ratio between belonging and striving? Who knows? But my bet is that belonging should always exceed striving, even though striving takes the risks needed to open new possibilities for belonging. In the absence of belonging, striving begins not to matter, loses meaning, and becomes absurd. Belonging is not just a cage which holds striving captive. Belonging can also legitimize and sustain striving. A society can commit to an ethos of creating conditions for belonging. What it can't do is make people belong. Nor

can they make themselves belong. That's not how belonging works. However well-intentioned, it's not a striving.

22. We can also think of belonging as need or attachment. Abraham Maslow's hierarchy of needs situates belonging (and love) as less fundamental than safety and physiological needs, but more basic than esteem and self-actualization. Attachment theory is normative in how it describes successful patterns of attachment favoring relationships. Both theories affirm our experience that belonging requires satisfaction and support by something external. Both theories imply that lack of belonging is a personal or social deficiency.

That would explain why belonging matters, but it doesn't explain why belonging is good for you besides satisfying your need to belong. That's a bit circular isn't it? Likewise, as attachment, belonging is synonymous with connection and bond. But that makes connection and bond (the more, the deeper, the more extensive, the better) the good rather than the lives bonded or connected. Belonging may be a need expressed in our attachments, and relationships matter, but why does belonging matter? What is this belonging which attachments and relationships supposedly accomplish and sustain, and why should we care about it?

23. Think of belonging as your life's second story. The first story would be analogous to a resume with a chronological listing of your tasks, accomplishments, and projects. Tributes and eulogies try to do justice to a life by extolling its merits and accomplishments: the first story. However, there is a *second story* of your life about how you experienced belonging or made it possible for others, and I would guess that it's not entirely unrelated to your history of strivings. This second story is not just about family, friends, and romance. Figuring out where and how you belong – and how others might belong - is a bigger story than that.

So, which is more important in life: striving or belonging? Without striving, life would not be possible. Without belonging, life would not matter. Who could make such a choice? What if we can't choose and want both? We would then shape our words, feelings, thoughts, and deeds to satisfy both narratives and invent all the ways in which we can individually or collectively strive and belong at the same time. When we're most intentional about life (pondering its meaning or direction), this is essentially what we're about.

24. But this belonging may sound too nebulous and free-floating. You insist on knowing exactly *where* you belong. Very well. Your life belongs in every other life. Every other life belongs in your life. The cosmos is a harsh place for fragile life, so life finds belonging within lives. Where else would you expect to find it?

Do the borders around lives make this sound impossible? Belonging trumps borders. Belonging trumps exclusion. Is that bizarre? Is it less bizarre than believing you can belong only inside your skin or on some special patch of ground? Is it less bizarre than supposing that belonging spreads out from you in ever fainter concentric ripples? This borderless belonging may make you feel intruded upon or spread too thin (maybe both), but your spirit never doubted that we're all in this together. You just thought we were stuck with each other. No, relationships provide the adhesive between lives, but belonging is life inter-situated within lives.

25. Rene Descartes closes his *Meditations* with a caution which applies to these meditations about belonging: *"...because the necessities of action frequently oblige us to come to determination before we have had leisure for so careful an examination, it must be confessed that the*

life of man is frequently obnoxious to error with respect to individual objects; and we must, in conclusion, acknowledge the weakness of our nature." [3] Meditate upon Toni Morrison's poem. Perhaps your belonging is not so strange and distant a place as you suppose.

> Whose house is this?
> Whose night keeps out the light
> In here?
> Say, who owns this house?
> It's not mine.
> I had another, sweeter, brighter
> With a view of lakes crossed in painted boats;
> Of fields wide as arms open for me.
> This house is strange.
> Its shadows lie.
> Say, tell me, why does its lock fit my key?
> ***(Toni Morrison, 1992)***

Welcome home.

CHAPTER 3

Animal Crackers

Whither Dither: A Duck's Special Day

One muggy Monday morning on duck pond, Dither Duck was moping and paddling in circles. He felt that he belonged nowhere and that nobody would ever invite him to belong. He wasn't an ugly duckling, as ducklings go, and duck pond wasn't such a bad place, but Dither was not sure about what to do with himself in this old pond. He could migrate, but he wanted more than a change of scene. He was

restless for real change, and he didn't know where to find it. Somehow that real change was connected with belonging, but it all seemed less likely every day. So, he dithered, aching to belong.

Suddenly, a water sprite appeared in a puff of environmentally-friendly second-hand pond mist. She announced that she felt sorry for Dither Duck and would grant him one wish. What did Dither want more than anything else? What would make his life complete?

"I want to belong!" cried Dither Duck. "I can't stand not belonging anywhere. Use your magic to take me off probation, out of limbo, and into warm and cozy belonging! Oh, I'd like change too – real change!"

The water sprite cocked her head sideways, to get some water out of her ear, looking puzzled. "But you do belong, Dither Duck. You always belonged and you always will. That's a done deal."

Dither Duck was stunned. He squawked: Mission accomplished?? I'm a duck, not a red-nosed reindeer! How can you call THIS magic? You've changed nothing! I'm still a misfit. Nobody gives me the time of day...well, except for you, but water sprites don't really count.

The sprite patiently explained, "Didn't you accept my blessing, Dither? You belong. Since you already belong, you still get one wish. Why not ask for invisibility? That's not nearly as empty as it looks, and nobody rejects the invisible..."

"NO! NO! NO! That's the whole problem! They *already* treat me like I'm invisible! It's like everyone in the world knows how to belong except for me."

"Look, Dither, if you have no wish, I have other wetland wishes to grant, so if you'll excuse me..."

Why should I just take your word that I already belong? What gives you the almighty authority to decide that?" Dither glared at the water sprite who was poised to dive back into the pond.

"I can breathe air or water, but I don't decide belonging, Dither." She sighed and said: "My blessing just splashes your belonging so that you'll notice it and stop paddling in circles. That's my wet gift to you. Anyone alive has enough authority to do that. You didn't need a water sprite."

Dither shouted: You can say that again! I could say 'I belong' all by myself!"

"So go ahead," said the water sprite. She shrugged and sat down on a lily to wait.

...and I can make myself belong anytime I want!
"Then why did you wish for it?" she asked.

Dither had no response, so he kept sniffling and paddling in circles. He finally said: What I need is a better pond, really. Someplace where I fit in. Point me in the right direction. Can you do that much?
"You belong in every life, and every life belongs in yours" said the sprite.
Dither Duck said: How could every life in the world possibly fit inside mine? My life isn't Noah's Ark. In fact, it's hardly even big enough for me. That's crazy!
The sprite assured Dither: "Your life has plenty of room."

And how can I possibly belong in every life? I can't be everywhere at once!
"Do you belong in the middle of duck pond?
Why not?
"Do you belong in the reeds?"
When I have to.
"Do you belong on the shore?"
When I want to.
"Do you belong flying over the wetlands?"

Why do you think I have wings?

"How do you belong in so many places?" asked the sprite. "Pond, reeds, and shore, and sky all belong in your life, don't they?"
Yes.
"How can they all belong in your life when it's so small?"

I get it. This is some kind of mystical revelation, right? I have to ponder your pearl of wisdom without snickering so that I can be enlightened?
"Well, no. *Life within lives* is how wetlands happen to work, and the whole biosphere basically handles belonging that way. It's odd that you have lived in a duck pond all your life and still don't believe it..."

Wait! Now I get it. If I say "I belong" and really believe it with all my heart, then no one can ever reject me, right?
"Dither, nobody much cares what a duck believes."
...but you just said...
"...And they can reject you anytime no matter what you believe."
So what good is this stupid belonging? What good are you to me in this pond?
"I'm not sure yet, Dither, but I think this might be where I belong."

Dither Duck wasn't impressed. This sprite should at least be sure about her own belonging. Besides, if he *somehow* belonged inside every life, he would need to be a guest – and a very good one at that, even within lives he feared. Did that include hungry foxes? If every life *somehow* belonged in his, Dither would have remodel his whole life (which was perfectly fine the way it was, apart from not belonging), to make room for all those lives.

Okay, let's suppose that I do belong like you say. Why don't I feel it in my bones? Why do I feel out of place? Why am I restless?

The sprite whispered in Dither's ear: "When you stop dithering; when you're ready for change –real change - ready to transform this muddy pond or be transformed by all those lives within yours, you won't need me to splash water on your belonging. You'll be wet all over."

Does that mean all of those other lives belong in my life too?

"Yes."

Even the hungry fox?

"Yes."

Dither Duck was disappointed: That worries me. Even worse, it means that there's nothing very special about belonging. Where's the satisfaction?

"It's no more special than life. Life only knows how to belong within lives. It never figured out how to belong anywhere else."

What's the point of migrating someplace if I already belong there? Heck, what's the point of doing anything at all?

"What's the point otherwise? Look, you don't seem ready for this gift."

Stop answering questions with questions! Besides, I have no gift for you.

"Yes you do. Please tell me that I belong."

Dither Duck was perplexed: You have doubts? But you're magical! Why on Earth do you need this duck to tell you that you belong?

"Because nobody can do that for themselves."

Well, if that's true, it's not very fair.

"Maybe not, but that's how belonging works."

Dither spoke carefully: Yes. Yes you do belong. Of course you belong. Why not?

"Thank you very much, Dither."

Dither Duck suddenly felt like crying again but he couldn't say why.

Instead, he got an idea: "Do I still get my one wish?"

"Yes. Wish for whatever your heart desires."

"I wish to belong in the hungry fox's life only when that fox belongs in my life."

The water sprite nodded. "That's shrewd. You might be paddling in another circle, but your wish is granted. It's a pleasure belonging in your life. I feel quite at home."

Likewise, I'm sure. Just don't get anything wet. Oh, and I *don't* want to ever hear that I don't belong!

"Stop quacking about not belonging anywhere. I don't like noisy guests."

Dither Duck pondered this. "I do feel better, but life within lives seems sticky and messy. My life would wind up terribly crowded and spread very thin. Don't get me wrong, I still want to belong very much, but wouldn't it be more sensible for a duck to simply belong inside his own feathers and nowhere else?

"How has that worked out for you so far?"

Ouch! I didn't see that coming. I doubt that I'm going to win this argument.

"When in doubt, duck."

THE END

Dither had barely enough courage to risk real change. Even the truth that he belonged was almost too much for him to accept. At the same

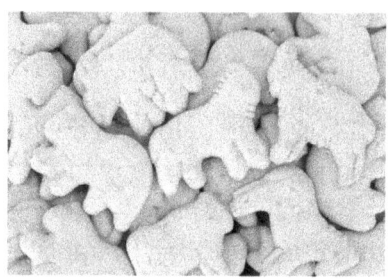

time, he experienced very little peace, justice, or love. He could not rest, life felt unfair, and nobody invited him to belong. The only meaningful gesture he makes is blessing the sprite in gratitude. Happily, that was enough.

Animals (humans included) strive and belong through meaningful activities. They move with purpose and hope. Swimming in busy circles like Dither Duck is not good enough. Protracted fretting and inactivity of any sort – captivity, doldrums or dithering – makes striving feel futile. It makes belonging feel out of reach. As it happens, without courage as a down payment, inactivity makes animals experience less peace, justice, or love. They can't explore to figure out what's true. What if the ways in which animals combine striving and belonging in activity make those values of courage, justice, peace, truth, and love tangible? If so, humans and other animals would share an ethos of core values. They already share the same capacities for movement. Perhaps they share much more.

Think of it this way: no matter how many different animals you get in a box of animal crackers, they all taste the same. *Homo sapiens* is missing from the box, so we'll bake one. Our cracker would taste exactly the same as the other animal crackers because we have the same animal capacities for movement: power, speed, strength, flexibility, balance, coordination, accuracy, agility, endurance, and stamina. Don't hunt for courage, justice, peace, truth, or love as prizes in the bottom of the box. They're already baked into each cracker.

I want to propose a theory about the core values of courage, justice, peace, truth, and love. The theory occurred to me in an unexpected way. After studying and sweating my way through different regimens of exercise and fitness, I realized that the movement values of these programs - power, speed, strength, flexibility, balance, coordination, accuracy, agility, endurance, and stamina – are capacities broader and deeper than physical movement.

For example, we speak of economic power, strong emotions, balanced lives, etc. without the necessity of leaping (!) into figurative language. I think we are spared leaping, *not* because these attributed capacities such as balance and agility are analogous to how we talk about muscular movement, but because these capacities were never merely physical movement in the first place. They are not simply the mechanics of how vertebrates use their muscles. They are capacities exercised in physical exertion but also in diverse dimensions of activity: moral, spiritual, economic, social, political, and institutional life express the same capacities. The animal crackers still have that slightly sweet taste.

Further, although humans pick which animals go into the box, human beings have no proprietary monopoly on animal capacities. We share them with every other animal. In fact, we learn about them by observing animals. These capacities have an aesthetic which we celebrate in sports and dance, and an everyday practicality grounded in the limitations and possibilities of muscular movement. Dance and sports have no proprietary monopoly on these capacities either. These capacities are features of all human activity. In fact, they're features of all *animal* activity.

What does this have to do with core values? Value is very much a ball in play, philosophically speaking. You can defend values as precious subjective preferences, useful evaluative categories, or transcendent and authoritative abstractions. You can be skeptical about values' authority, universality, or enduring nature.

There are competing theories about the origin and evolution of values which societies construct and affirm. I am grabbing the ball to argue that our animal capacities exercised in activity are not merely a context for value but enable us to experience five values in particular: courage, justice, peace, truth, and love:

1. We experience the feel of courage, justice, peace, truth, and love in the exercise of our capacities for activity. We find the best of our humanity within this shared animality.

2. These values are encountered not as personal belief nor as social wordplay, but rather as kinesthetic challenges of meaningful activity.

3. We experience core values of courage, justice, peace, truth, and love as living values according to how we combine certain capacities in our activities.

4. A sedentary society that normalizes inactivity and problematizes activity makes our experience of these values reduced, muted, uncertain and compromised.

One surprising corollary of this approach to values is that non-human animals "have" exactly the same core values as human animals do because they share the same mechanical challenges as vertebrates actively moving. You might object that only humans can think about values. That's true, but are animal crackers any less sweet and munchy because you don't think about them?

At this point, I'm relying on my philosophical intuition, but I think you can confirm these intuitions for yourself. They aren't arbitrary or whimsical, nor are they delivered from on high. I provide my best guess below about how we combine capacities to experience values, and try to give this experience some texture by guesstimating how much striving and belonging go into these value experiences.

We experience **courage** by exercising power within the urgent constraints of speed. We know that speed makes exercise of power risky. Power invests (or simply gambles) other capacities to make a time-sensitive difference. We call this wager of our capacities "mustering" courage. I don't think we claim to "muster" any other value. Think of power as striving and think of speed as being where and when we belong. Does that mean that every exercise of power and speed provides an experience of courage? No. That's where aesthetics comes into play. If you think my deed was courageous (and not foolhardy), you pay attention to what I'm wagering, at risk to myself, and to the situation's speed constraints. It doesn't exhaust the historical and cultural meaning of "courage" but it does ground the value in two of our animal capacities. It's no coincidence that we choose certain animals such as lions to represent human courage.

What capacities do we combine to experience justice? I suggest that we experience **justice** as strength against resistance within the flexible reach of our values and rules. You might object that no one can "experience" an abstract concept. However, before the value is reified, culturally endorsed, and given intellectual "shelf life" as an ideal and abstraction, we develop a "feel" for the value in our activities. Strength and flexibility seem the capacities most at stake in our experience of justice. Of course, strength by itself is not justice. Neither is flexibility. However, together they give a sense of "just rightness" or "enough" which we learn from our experience of reach and resistance.

I thought carefully about peace from a kinesthetic perspective. My intuition is that we experience **peace** whenever our activities equally balance and coordinate. Of course, the intuition that balance is part of peace is not new. However, if peace were only a matter of achieving balance, peace would look fragile and vulnerable to any imbalance. But, for peace, balance is not an end in itself. Balance makes sense – and is more resilient – when matched by coordination. Likewise, coordination manipulates and blends diverse movements into a meaningful activity, but without balance relative to some base of support, coordination is hard to sustain with confidence or necessary complexity. We think of peace activism as striving to coordinate fragmented or conflicting elements, but it's equally a matter of restoring and finding anew a society's sense of balance. Together, they make peace live.

You probably think of truth as a value quite independent of our capacities for activity. If so, I invite you to consider whether truth has "feel" to it. We feel the dynamics of **truth** as striving for accuracy with enough agility to change position or direction as dictated by changing truth conditions. We usually start talking about truth with dualities such as subjective v. objective or absolute v. relative. Keep in mind that capacities for accuracy and agility are not just about physical nimbleness.

The most challenging of these five values is **love.** Although it sounds dogged and dreary, I think we experience love (as a value) first in our endurance and stamina. That's not the same thing as feeling love, of course. But I think we learn to trust love's credibility as we test these capacities. Think of endurance as learning to belong in relationship with suffering. Think of stamina as hope and perseverance. These capacities don't define or exhaust love, but love needs intuitive credibility before we risk feeling and committing to it as a value. When we see animals endure with stamina for the sake of their young or partners (or owners), we identify emotionally with their experience. That's not anthropomorphizing. That's not projection. Animal crackers taste the same whether you're guarding a nest or putting up with a friend.

"Capacity" as our metaphysical category may sound like Aristotle's idea of potential *(potentia).* You might visualize some empty container or placeholder, probably with a certain size and shape. However, living capacities grow and are transformed as they are exercised. A capacity is not a pure structure or form. A capacity is not an inert actualization-ready potential, nor a bland disposition to move in this way or that. You can describe skills and habits that way, but capacities are meta-patterns of activity which muscular vertebrates combine and bring to life.

It's not accurate to call them abilities. For example, I may have less ability than you, though we exercise the same capacity. The animal crackers in your box are bigger than mine, but we have the same kinds of crackers. And they taste the same.

However, these capacities are not ideas or categories. I'm arguing that we have a kinesthetic feel for each of the five values - courage, justice, peace, truth, and love – as we combine two or more of our capacities. Like Pythagoras, I'm giving you some ratios, because our capacities combine striving and belonging in distinctive proportions. The percentages are my best intuition about the ratio of striving to belonging for the "feel" of a particular value. The arguments for these intuitions are what Part Two of this book is about.

1. *Courage* exercises power within speed constraints which may risk life and limb to make a difference and open new ways of belonging.
   Power - 80% striving Speed – 20% belonging

2. Justice exercises strength against resistance and is flexible enough to bend rules.
   Flexibility – 60% striving Strength – 40% belonging

3. Peace is an individual's or community's coordination of activities on the move while balanced relative to a base of support.
   Coordination – 50% striving Balance – 50% belonging

4. Truth is an accuracy which is nimble enough to change direction or position as dictated by conditions.
    Accuracy – 40% striving Agility – 60% belonging

5. Love becomes credible through our enduring relationship with suffering, given hope and direction by stamina
    Stamina – 20% Endurance 80%

Assigning numbers can make content and their relationships appear falsely definitive. Rest assured that this is no kabbalah, but only a tool to show how ten of your capacities pair up to give you an experience of these five values. You may object to how I describe these values or disagree about whether a capacity is about striving or belonging. Keep in mind that I'm describing the kinesthetic *feel* of these values rather than defining them as abstractions or subjective commitments.

I think that power, strength, coordination, accuracy, and stamina are mainly *strivings* which transform internal or external environments. Speed, flexibility, balance, agility, and endurance are capacities for *belonging* that open us to transformation. Combine a capacity to belong with a capacity to strive in distinctive ways and proportions, and you get an experiential "feel" for how otherwise distant and purely abstract values of love, justice, peace, truth, and courage are lived in your concrete activities. Striving vs. belonging is not just another duality. It's a dance in which you mix and combine your capacities to create something new: the experience of living values.

These ten capacities are familiar to exercise science, [4]but I present them here as something much more than physical skills. Think of them as basic and deeper human capacities, which are also generic animal capacities. As homage to Aristotle's ten categories, I've chosen ten capacities. However, these are not mere objects of apprehension. They are capacities basic to all vertebrate animals. The percentages are my best intuition about the ratio of striving to belonging in the experience of a particular value. You may disagree about those percentages, or about whether a particular capacity counts as "striving" or "belonging," but consider this a kinesthetic chapter in our phenomenology of values. This is not our encounter with values as abstractions or subjective commitments. This encounter is the experience of our capacities in meaningful activity.

I am not quite certain whether this approach belongs in a particular philosophical tradition. It's a major bypass around the dualism of mind and body, but it's not about embodiment, Nietzsche's "will to power," nor is it pragmatism tailored for a gym. It's not a holism about the relationship between parts and a whole. Striving reminds me of Henri Bergson's concept of life as "élan vital" but vitalism begs the question of what makes the élan "vital." I am looking at life as transformative striving and belonging, which at least gives us more to argue about. It's not the last word on the meaning of life, but it's a way of understanding life which rightly includes belonging and makes transformation an everyday reality of activity.

You could call this *process philosophy*, but this process is not change, but an alteration which we call *transformation* (real change, making a difference, or becoming new). Like change, transformation is process with duration and dynamics, but you don't describe the transformative meaning of striving and belonging by saying how much or little change happened or even what sort of change is involved. As you know, a great deal of change can mean little or no transformation (plus ça change, plus c'est la même chose). But you can also think of genuine and palpable transformation which meant very little change. Sometimes, making a difference or being transformed is simply not about changing things. Transformation can be a critical juncture or a point where nothing will ever be the same, despite the same old changes or no change at all.

This is an ethos for transformation, but it's not an ethics. This ethos is lodged between ethics and aesthetics. You could call it dynamic axiology (an operational theory of values), but I'm considering only five values. Unlike ethics, this ethos does not consider motive, consequence, principle, entitlement, or obligation. This ethos is about capacities, not choice and intentionality. You may think of political and social philosophy as the right home for belonging, but we have much to do before working out a politics for transformation and belonging.

I'm not reducing courage, justice, peace, truth, and love to how we experience movement. I think that kinesthetic experience is the locus, but not the totality, of these values' intuitive meaning. Don't worry about whether moral, spiritual, political, and mental capacities are more real or less real than physical capacities, because the animal crackers all taste equally sweet. You can take Plato's high road and treat values as somewhere above physical movement, but you have to dismiss your concrete intuitive experience of these values on the move. If you take the pragmatic path and declare that how you experience movement and its consequences is the only real meaning for these values, you make your values relative to your subjective experience.

Both roads are dead ends. I know that thinking in terms of capacities and activity is hard to do without some specific movement-context such as physical therapy or coaching, but worry less about which animals are in the box, how many are left, and how big they are, and simply appreciate that there is plenty of variety.

For example, ask like Pontius Pilate, "What is truth?" and typically the hunt begins for some elusive animal. Is it in the stars, in the dirt, or in your heart? Was it ever anywhere at all? Dwell instead with your intuitions about what truth feels like (and how startling to acknowledge that truth should have a feel at all!) and you needn't go truth-hunting. You immediately speak of "hitting the mark" or "ringing true" "making contact" or some equivalent tactile "just-rightness". Whenever you try to move with accuracy and agility, you're "moving in truth" perhaps towards a moving target, but then you're moving as well. This all may sound very far removed from propositions and truth conditions, but when you confront skepticism about whether truth is possible, it's good to be reminded that truth means activity: nimbleness as much as verisimilitude.

The box of animal crackers is empty now, but you bake up a new box every day as you swing into activity. Here's the argument again:

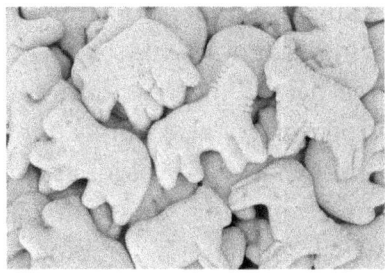

1. We experience the feel of courage, justice, peace, truth, and love in the exercise of our capacities for activity. We find the best of our humanity within this shared animality.

2. These values are encountered not as personal belief nor as social wordplay, but rather as kinesthetic challenges of meaningful activity.

3. We experience core values of courage, justice, peace, truth, and love as living values according to how we combine certain capacities in our activities.

4. A sedentary society which normalizes inactivity and problematizes activity makes our experience of these values reduced, muted, uncertain and compromised.

Does (4) imply that you should never be skeptical about courage, justice, peace, truth, and love? No. But it suggests that a culture of protracted and self-justifying sedentary inactivity makes meaningful activity and belonging seem impractical, out of reach, supererogatory, or else simply not worth the effort. Does (4) imply that these values are absolute and unchanging? No. If anything, we would expect the diverse ways in which animal life combines capacities for activity to mean exactly the opposite. Does it mean that these values are universal? Yes, though these values turn out to be *far more univer*sal than any human-centered axiology might suppose. Our species does put its distinctive spin on these capacities and core values. And *homo sapiens* is the only species with words. But it never really had the last word. Maybe that's reason for hope.

Why then are we uncertain about the standing of these values or whether they belong in our lives? You can think of many reasons, but in the next chapter, I draw your attention to a surprising and unexpected reason. Please remain seated.

CHAPTER 4
Please remain seated

> **WARNING**
> Before commencing any program of sustained physical inactivity, consult your physician. Sedentary living doubles the likelihood of stroke and coronary artery disease, making it as risky as smoking, high cholesterol, or high blood pressure. If unaccustomed to sitting for extended periods, you may experience weak muscles, low bone density, high cholesterol, hyperglycaemia, a rapid resting heart rate, mental decline, mood disorders, and obesity. Start slowly and increase inactivity gradually. If you experience drowsiness, difficulty in concentration, or craving for stimulation, discontinue inactivity immediately.

Please remain seated

I made up this gag warning, and I realize that you might not share my sense of humor. So, I don't expect a laugh, but, for a split second, experience normalized prolonged inactivity in an abrupt and unsettling way like vertigo or a lingering photoflash on your retina. *Just how the hell did your life turn into a shopping mall parking lot?* Don't immediately moralize about couch potatoes as though the question is merely about how much or how little you move. It's about what you now think inactivity *means* when you've long since forgotten that you're inactive. Let's say that you belong inactive in your chair to read this book. Consider that, in our culture, the practice of sitting means more than a convenient way to read. It means a silently endorsed open-ended entitlement to "rest," which, unlike real rest, makes you feel evermore tired.

I want to convince you that you belong – and feel a sense of belonging – in activity. However much or little activity is open to you, that's where you're ripe and ready for transformation. Inactivity, however much or little, is not the kind of duration in which you belong and feel belonging. So, if you live in a mostly inactive and seldom active culture, your belonging is going to suffer. You might even doubt that it exists. In activity, things are transformed; you might fall down or land on your feet; you might endure or give up; you might hit the mark or miss it. None of this is summoned by inactivity. That doesn't make inactivity bad. But numbed and numbing inactivity can make transformation feel difficult or even impossible.

You agree that prolonged inactivity is hazardous, but you still sit and go on sitting. And so do we all. Please remain seated. Don't fight for your life or flee from inactivity. Animals freeze until it's safe to move, but your inactivity is not playing possum. You remain still in one place (or in a string of places) indefinitely not to protect yourself, but only because inactivity feels so familiar and socially unobjectionable that it successfully masquerades as *your life*. You might shift to another empty space in life's mall parking lot without thinking about leaving the lot. And so do we all. Like Plato's prisoners in the cave, we remain seated for the shadow show, but we must begin where are, even as we only now remember the function of the parking brake.

In other words, living with an open-ended invitation to inactivity is hazardous not just to your health, but also for your belonging. Belonging happens in activity as you risk vulnerability to *transformation*. By contrast, prolonged inactivity

means vulnerability to changes, many of them negative: less energy, less inclination to move, and more justification for not moving. Some of the changes are positive: entertainment, convenience, and relief for the feet, but whether the changes are positive or negative, inactivity is *not* about striving or belonging. Inactivity also has tremendous self-justifying inertia. You don't need to explain this inactivity because it's perfectly (too perfectly) normal. In fact, it's activity that now requires a reason. You have somehow become the single animal on Earth that thinks it needs a reason to move. (Now you may laugh).

Do I mean that you can't belong if you're inactive? No. But activity is where you experience belonging. Whatever humanity you hope to find in belonging, you discover it in mobile animality. Think of belonging not as entitlement to proprietary inertia but as actively living within your capacities of power, speed, strength, flexibility, endurance, stamina, balance, coordination, agility, and accuracy. Every animal feels belonging through these generic capacities. You and your community are no exception.

Before we examine these capacities and what they contribute to an ethos of transformation, let's begin in the middle of our culture where ongoing inactivity is not just acceptable but often expected, and activity is problematized and considered in need of justification. Here are six ways to release the parking brake and get us out of intellectual, physical, and cultural inactivity and into belonging:

1. **Don't fight inactivity by becoming more active.**

2. **You are not an object at rest. You are probably not even a rested person.**

3. **You have enough of these capacities to make a difference.**

4. **Seek belonging for your humanity within the best of your animality.**

5. **Don't abandon or out-source your own capacities for transformation.**

6. **Think of yourself as *already* very much in motion, from the inside out.**

**

1. **Don't fight inactivity by becoming more active.**

If prolonged self-justifying inactivity undermines your sense of belonging and only makes you vulnerable to negative changes, it would seem that you should do the opposite and become more active. However, that alone doesn't work. You can't make yourself or anyone else belong simply by being more active. The "solution" for sedentary living is not more activity, but readiness for transformation within activity. Call it "beginner's mind on the move." Your activity is not just resolve and striving but dynamic openness to qualitative changes.

Those changes may be simple – you want to feel enjoyment of life. You want to help. You want to do something worthwhile or at least interesting. "Being open" sounds passive, but intentional receptivity isn't limpness. You don't just need movement. You need to actively transform into what you're meant to be, what your activity is supposed to be, as you strive to transform environments. Think: what draws you into activity where you both strive and belong in satisfying ways? What everyday transformation are you ready for in your life? Then you'll summon all the power, speed, strength, flexibility, endurance, stamina, balance, coordination, accuracy and agility you need.

2. You are not an object at rest. You are probably not even a rested person.

Don't think of yourself as an object at rest. This is not about Newton's First Law of Motion. That law states that *an object at rest stays at rest, and an object in motion stays in motion with the same speed and direction, unless acted upon by an unbalanced force.* You may be sitting, but you are absolutely not inert like a mannequin. In fact, you are a bundle of incipient pulsating movement and rushing energy subjected to unnatural constraint and restraint. No wonder sitting makes you tired! Respond to your parking lot not by launching into unceasing movement, but by honoring, unpacking, and extending that movement bundle into your life and the world.

Nor are you a racecar waiting for the starting flag. You may think of your movement as a single linear variable which can be measured from zero (couch potato) to 10 (running a marathon), but no animal is ever at zero. Mind you, some come close. The three-fingered sloth (*Bradypus torquatus*) scarcely moves. The arboreal three-fingered sloth rarely comes down from hanging on a tree branch, except to answer the call of nature once a week. The sloth is motionless enough that green algae grows in its fur. Good camouflage perhaps, but phlegmatic metabolism almost disqualifies it as a mammal. Still, the sloth's skillful way of (barely) moving is how it belongs in movement.

More than making nests or marking territory, animals feel belonging through movement they've practiced and learned. I invite you that you feel belonging this way. Skillful movement learned through practice, training, and feedback, turns your spaces into meaningful concourses. For example, ducking to avoid a blow is an unthinking reaction, but it becomes skilled when you're a boxer capable of ducking adroitly under pressure. Disciplined movement is more transformative than good habits, not because it's more deliberative, premeditated, or even more intelligent, but because we pour more of ourselves into learning, perfecting, and combining our capacities for activity.

3. You have enough of these capacities to make a difference.

You may have a fundamental misgiving about this talk of power, speed, and strength, *et al.* You lament that you really don't have much of these capacities. You have compared yourself to more able-bodied others or to more able-bodied versions of yourself, and you come up short. All this talk of capacities simply rubs your nose in these personal deficits. All is not lost. You can deal with this misgiving in several ways. First, these capacities tend to improve only with practice and training. How much do you really want to use your capacities?

Second, effective use of capacities is about transformation, not making big changes. This is not about how strong, fast, or coordinated you are. This is not about making a meteoric impact, but about using those capacities (which were never just physical skills anyway) either to make a propitious and well-timed difference or to make yourself ready and willing to undergo transformation. You may lack mobility and mobility may be painful, but, with less to work with, you will be more creative, selective, and judicious about your activities. That care increases the odds that your exercise of capacities for activity will be transformative.

Finally, recognize that assuming ownership of your capacities runs against the grain of a culture which dismisses, out-sources, or professionalizes capacities. It runs against the grain of a culture in which no one moves without a good reason. It runs against the grain of an "ableist" society which lionizes the able-bodied but never the able-spirited and able-hearted. Pat yourself on the back for progress you make, not by becoming "more able," but by simply believing in your own activity. The categories of "able" and "disabled" don't have much meaning or relevance here because moving with courage, justice, peace, truth, and love is enough of a challenge for anyone. And you have enough capacities to make a difference.

4. Seek belonging for your humanity in the best of your animality.

You belong, therefore you matter. I invite you to experience your belonging through your active animality. You have animal strength, power, speed, flexibility, *et al.*, and that's enough capacity to feel belonging day in and day out. Don't try to belong by joining a group. Join in activity. Don't judge your capacities. Live and work with them. Don't outsource your natural power and speed to machines as if fast cars and powerful engines are the only fit repositories for power and speed. *At least your power and speed is alive!*

Don't live as though your capacities belong only to dancers and athletes. When you're in inactivity doldrums, this out-sourcing of movement capacity is exactly what you'd expect. Nevertheless, your stretch, reach, timing, bounce, nimbleness, persistence, push, pull, and grip are your skill mosaic for making sense and concourse out of life. Exercising these capacities matters for animals (human and nonhuman) more than any cherished, defended, or sought-after place. An animal restricted to its favorite place still experiences boredom and captivity, not belonging. Place is no substitute for concourse. You may think of airports and bus stations when you hear "concourse." Think of strolling with a friend or weaving through a crowd. Keep weaving those concourses together and you might wind up with community.

5. Don't abandon or out-source your own capacities for transformation.

In the dithering stretches of inactivity, you gradually lose confidence in your own capacities. It is replaced by resignation about how you're slow, weak, stiff, clumsy, bumbling, stumbling, and tend to give in, give up, or give out after brief exertion. "Skill" and "capacity" can be intimidating words, especially if your inactivity is not chosen, unfamiliar, unfair, or seems inescapable. Just as I cautioned against treating belonging as something external to you (like the shadows on the wall of the prisoners' cave), I'm cautioning against thinking of your birthright animal capacities as proprietary possessions of (other) animals, machines, or people in sports and the performing arts.

Remember that these are your distinctive vulnerability to training and experience. They represent all your sustained, systematic or disciplined engagement in activity. You might act as though you have no capacities ("I could never do X"), but that's just normalized inactivity talking. People also act as though they don't belong or could never belong. Consider how "I could never do X" and "I could never belong" are deeply linked. Skepticism about your basic capacities and prospects for meaningful activity means that you're less inclined to be active. If you experience belonging in activity, then belonging is bound to suffer during protracted inactivity. Yes, you still belong (and you always did), but you're more likely to forget that you belong. You're less likely to have confidence about how you can belong. If you care more about striving, this might not matter to you – at first. But without belonging, striving devolves from quest into farce.

So, I am not scolding you to go outside, learn a sport, get up and exercise, stop watching T.V., burn calories or make time to move around. Getting active is not the point. With presumptive hospitality, I invite you to change your default setting from inactivity to concourse-making, value-generating, and personally satisfying activity. My welcome includes adults and kids, coaches for municipal and community sport leagues, professional athletes in retirement, or anyone who feels trapped in a cocoon of inactivity and has lost confidence in their movement possibilities. Especially if you've lost some range of movement which you can't recover, take heart that you belong in a world rich with movement possibilities, and your grace is a big part of that wealth. You belong, and you always did.

6. Think of yourself as already very much in motion, from the inside out.

Dancer Erin Manning makes an extended argument in *Relationscapes – Movement, Art, and Philosophy* (2012) that our movement doesn't just happen in space but actually creates space (what I call "concourse.") She describes movement as: "*...an acceleration of the movement which has already begun. The movement within becomes a movement without, not internal-external, but folding and bridging in an intensity of preacceleration. This means you are never stopped. To move is to engage the potential inherent in the preacceleration that embodies you.*[5]"

This is not ceaseless exhausting striving. This is readiness as "preaccelerated movement." You are a myriad of movement and activity barely contained by your skin. Human movement is not simply a one-dimensional linear quality measured from zero to exhaustion. Manning draws upon philosophers such as Whitehead, Bergson, and Deleuze to describe this incipient movement, but, however we describe it, let's first acknowledge that we are already full of movement. How then will we honor it?

Please remain seated

Belonging allows us to *normalize activity and problematize inactivity*, so it helps that animal life is stacked in favor of movement. Each of us unfolds incipient movement on many levels, however inactive we seem on the surface. Each human body is plastic rhythm packed with intensity. Perhaps you don't feel like a bouncing Tigger or jack-in-the-box ready to spring free. You prefer to stop, smell the roses, and meditate. Why budge? What about meditation and blessed stillness?

As practitioners will attest, even the Zen discipline of sitting meditation (as opposed to sitting around) isn't non-movement or inactivity. It's an impressive coordination of countless micro-movements together against distractions and temptations to lose patience, posture, and inner balance. Standing, whether loitering or in a queue, isn't really motionless. When you stand, you're not pretending to be a mannequin. Standing is actually a kind of two-step micro swaying. As animals, we unfold movement every second, and we're happiest with good ways to continue and improvise on that movement.

If movement is where belonging works, why is so much of our daily life sedentary inactivity? We can speculate. Perhaps, as Dr. Steven Robbins argues, sitting was normalized in the West during the Renaissance when footwear became widespread in

Europe. Constricting footwear made prolonged weight-bearing activity uncomfortable, resulting in a need to sit or recline. That practice began a nasty and negative feedback loop leading to rigidity and muscle atrophy, making weight-bearing activity all the more uncomfortable. Sedentary inactivity then became addictive and normalized.[6]

Whatever the cause for normalized inactivity, it tends to dull our sense of belonging. I once brought three servals to my classroom for environmental ethics students who sat in circle on the floor. The students had been debating how to relate to wild animals. These agile wild cats sprang from their crates and immediately checked out doors, hopped on the tables, and investigated the windows. (All had been carefully locked.) The servals cared more about movement possibilities than meeting students. The wild cats clearly felt belonging as they made a concourse while the sitting students suddenly felt out of place!

Remember being a kid? You didn't just take up space. You made concourses. Why run? Why *not* run?

Please remain seated

Perhaps your movements now seem perfunctory, habitual, and functional (if you prefer, carefully chosen, effective, and no-nonsense). Or your surroundings don't invite you to belong very much. If so, you'll feel that you don't know what to do with yourself in those places. If you aspire to be a mover in the world, consider first how you move. Heck, consider whether you move. Manning refers to this as auto-action. No matter how you feel about your abilities, competence, or adequacy, you move with skill. You belong. You plus walking equals concourse. How can you tell if normalized inactivity keeps you from being open to transformation? Put away your GPS, and answer these questions:

- Do you feel that "where you live" is first and foremost someone else's world rather than your world? Do you look for permission cues to move there? Or do you feel that it's nobody's world and that no movement, however skillful, will help you to belong there?

- Do you assume that you're always starting from zero when you make a move?

- Do you feel that your movement is optional unless you have a good, very good, or downright compelling reason for moving?

- Are the words "inconvenient," "uncomfortable" and "time-consuming" decisive objections to any proposed movement?

Suppose that you answer "yes" to most or all of these questions. What are the stakes for belonging? Stop asking "Why should I move?" Ask "Why on Earth am I not moving?" Sustained inactivity is a key indicator for disease and early death. In the cocoon of normalized inactivity, you will spend your time reacting to other people's movements. That's stressful. Also, you will not make positive changes in the world where you want to belong – not if they require active skillful movement. That's sloth (and not the cute furry kind). And you are less likely to object strenuously to negative features of the world so long as they allow you to remain in your chair. Perhaps the meek will inherit the Earth, but the inert will inherit only their inertia.

Lastly, you won't make any concourses for belonging. There's nothing wrong with resting from activity. But "rest" no isolated abstraction. It's in relationship with activity. A life of normalized inactivity can have very little refreshing rest. Can you just remain still? Sitting or standing with intentional stillness is a movement discipline. Those intentional choices are qualitatively different than hanging around as a default. I think we each know this, but when we start avoiding weight-bearing activity (physically or spiritually), that's dithering, not belonging.

The lesson is not to beat ourselves up about inactivity. The lesson is to know that all life belongs and that you honor and experience and develop that belonging in activity. Think of yourself as so packed with incipient movement that you can hardly think of any compelling reason for prolonged inactivity. That's not a St. Vitus dance of nonstop striving waiting to happen. It's activity into which you can pour yourself with joy, intelligence, purpose, and risk.

Erin Manning notes: *"We can think of movement in at least two ways:*

1. *I enter a room and see that room as preexisting me. I walk across the room, drawing an imaginary line that cuts the space.*

2. *My movement creates the space I will come to understand as "the room." The room is defined as my body + the environment, where the environment is an atmospheric body. Without that particular moving body that particular environment does not exist."*[7]

You Always Belonged and You Always Will

What I mean by movement creating *concourse* is Manning's second option. Your activity makes the room, and it's not a dance, not a party, until you show up. But don't expect us to sit around waiting for you. ☺

CHAPTER 5
Rethinking Discipline

When I share my blessing "you belong," you needn't be situated in your most congenial spot. Please enjoy this blessing wherever you happen to be. *You belong where you live,* because your belong-ing is less about where you happen to live and more about whether you're ready to be transformed in some way. No, you need not undergo metamorphosis or conversion. But when you undergo difficult changes in how you think, feel, and interact which are for the better, when you put your life someplace you didn't expect, and yet you feel that you always belonged there, that's real change or "transformation."

If your changes only freshen up or improve your status quo, they may be worthwhile but they do not transform. Nor will those positive changes affirm that you belong. Some places may be more hospitable to belong than others, but instead of fixating on those places, wield your amazing capacities of power, speed, strength, flexibility, endurance, stamina, balance, coordination, accuracy, and agility. You don't need more or better capacities. Practice them in diverse activities which open you to possible transformation. The engine of transformation is discipline.

You may think of *disciplines* as branches of knowledge or as rules for children and soldiers, enforced by punishment. However, I invite you to think of disciplines also as meaningful domains of practice and training through which your capacities allow you to belong. Learning, practicing, and enjoying a discipline honors your belonging. This is not self-discipline to grab your bootstraps and make yourself do something. Nor is this conforming to a disciplinary regime. What's confusing is that we use all these meanings of "discipline" to describe our activities. You may practice and receive training to climb rocks (**a discipline**) by conforming to expectations and best practices (**disciplinary submission**) but feel the need for **self-discipline** in climbing when you're afraid, discouraged, or tired. I'm focusing on discipline as trained and practiced beginner's activity because I believe that this way for life to belong in lives is neglected. As such, I'll argue for these three claims about discipline:

1. **Discipline as commitment to and capacity for real change fosters belonging. Belonging is the most compelling sort of authority.**

2. **Discipline as tool of power and authority fosters conformity and compliance. Its purpose is to control and to dictate terms of belonging. We resist by increasing domains of leisure and casual living outside the borders of disciplinary power.**

3. **Paradoxically, discipline as commitment to and capacity for real change isolates you from your surroundings so that you may belong anew.**

Dancers submit to rehearsal. Athletes warm up to be ready to play. You're not a dancer or an athlete? You're a klutz? Then you've exercised these capacities (which were never merely physical skills) elsewhere:

learning to play a musical instrument, practicing facilitation of small groups, gardening, dancing, hunting, acquiring a second language, coming up with excuses, or another activity of yours which combines striving and belonging in satisfying and rewarding ways. You learn that capacity's feel in physical movement, but the capacity has a much larger life. Whatever suffering you've endured, your capacity to endure is not limited to those experiences nor is it limited to one kind of endurance. In fact, I'll argue that the distinctive ways in which we mix striving and belonging give us a feel for courage, justice, peace, truth, and love. At the same time, we experience those values lived as disciplined activity, transforming people, groups, and situations.

However, you may still feel stuck in the inactivity doldrums like a "painted ship on a painted ocean," where winds have been calm so long that it's hard to believe in your own movement possibilities. In maritime lore, the windless doldrums above and below the equator are called "horse latitudes." One story attributes that name to the desperate measure of casting horses overboard when they could no longer be cared for. So, if your horsepower has been jettisoned, you need to rescue those capacities, one at a time. Another story attributes "horse latitudes' to a ritual of sailors making a stuffed horse onboard to toss overboard when the mariners had worked off their "horse debt" from advanced wages. Maybe you see activity only as a debt to pay so that you can then do nothing. I invite you to think of activity in other ways as well.

1. Discipline as commitment to and capacity for real change fosters belonging. Belonging is the most compelling sort of authority.

If you still believe that activity matters for your own humanity, I invite you to think anew about discipline as a way of belonging and not just as punishment or control. Let's begin with the capacities of power  and speed. Forget racecars, powerful engines, and other technological marvels of power and speed. I'm referring to *your own* power and speed. The maximal force you can apply in minimal time is your power. Your ability to minimize time for repeated movement is the extent of your speed. You've got both. Every time you apply power where needed (and you only need enough to make a difference), you belong. Your capacity for speed doesn't mean moving fast, by the way. It means the ability to control your speed across a wide range. Successfully slowing down is as much a capacity for speed as deliberately speeding up.

Suppose a child learns to play soccer and invests considerable time, effort, practice, and training to maneuver with greater speed and power. Rules of the sport and the child's skill give feints, footwork, and turning with the ball skillful meaning and help the child to belong in the game. But outside the borders of sports and games, in the terrain of everyday life, human speed and power are rarely acknowledged, expected, or approved. ("Stop running!") Speed and power are externalized as features of fast cars, powerful interests, fast-paced life, etc. For adults, externalizing power and speed is so ingrained that these capacities become impersonal and virulently anti-personal. Life itself seems to have speeded up beyond reason, and power seems to reside everywhere but in oneself. Power and speed are experienced as brutal discipline externally forced upon people.

2. **Discipline as tool of power and authority fosters conformity and compliance. Its purpose is to control and to dictate terms of belonging. We resist by increasing domains of leisure and casual living outside the borders of disciplinary power.**

Michel Foucault famously argued in *Discipline and Punish* (1976) that, in the modern era, discipline seeps into and shapes our institutional and personal lives as imposed and ingratiating structures and mechanisms of power and control. Clare O'Farrell provides a concise and accurate summary of Foucault's view of discipline:

> Discipline is a mechanism of power which regulates the behavior of individuals in the social body. This is done by regulating the organization of space (architecture, etc.) of time (timetables) and people's activity and behavior (drills, posture, movement). It is enforced with the aid of complex systems of surveillance. Foucault emphasizes that power is not discipline; rather discipline is simply one way in which power can be exercised. He also uses the term 'disciplinary society', discussing its history and the origins and disciplinary institutions such as prisons, hospitals, asylums, schools, and army barracks. Foucault also specifies that when he speaks of a 'disciplinary society' he does not mean a 'disciplined society.[8]

Foucault's discipline-imposing framework seems to aggressively push any meaningful ethos of belonging out of the picture. But, as noted, *'disciplinary'* is not the same as *'disciplined.'* In a disciplinary all-seeing panopticon society, discipline is the external (and ultimately internalized) enemy of belonging. It ensures conformity and holds belonging hostage to compliance. Disciplined activity is vulnerability to transformation, not authority.

That said, people resist disciplinary compliance in work, school, and other public activities by staking out parcels of leisure which free from disciplinary expectations. Call this foot-dragging resistance goofing off, hanging out, or social bonding, but people aren't merely reacting to and escaping from disciplinary expectations. The resistance hides a deeper hunger for belonging and real change. Even when resistance succeeds and people have no idea of what to do with themselves, their undefined hope endures.[9]

Disciplined activity can mean intense training or casual play. Discipline can be grudging and passive compliance or autonomous and packed with dedicated purpose. However, the common denominator for this kind of activity is your tradeoff: isolation from your surroundings in exchange for reclaimed belonging or belonging on new terms.

Many exercise regimens began in military boot camps enforcing physical discipline, but we should not commit the genealogical fallacy of reducing movement's meaning to its origins. Disciplined movement may be dictated by external authority but it can be a way to experience belonging. You feel on track, in rhythm, and even graceful. When that activity captivates you to the point of complete personal investment, you feel belonging and the possibility of transformation. Even if you're doing the same jumping jacks as everyone else, conformity is not the point.

Suppose that I want to get in shape (whatever that means to me), but you decide to take up rock climbing. You join an indoor climbing gym and learn to belay and partner with other climbers scaling vertical surfaces so that you can go on outdoor excursions. We both devote considerable time, energy, sweat, and resolve. For me, "getting in shape" means worshipping that weird social construct of "fitness" propped up by compelling ever-distant icons of bodily perfection.

You learn climbing skills. Your rock climbing is *disciplined* practice and training, but my striving for the fuzzy blessed state of fitness is mostly *disciplinary*. I have internalized disciplinary mandates. You invest yourself in practice and training. I work out in the face of temptations to do otherwise. You simply try to get better at climbing. I buy into the disciplinary demands of "fitness culture," but you climb and get better at it. You do so with your belay partner as a matter of safety, and I would guess that both of you feel more belonging in your physical exertions than I do. In fact, the owner of my gym probably bets on my belonging deficit to ensure turnover and new memberships.

Put it this way: I subject myself to disciplinary expectations but you pour yourself into a discipline. Discipline fosters belonging because, within its parameters, you know in new and challenging ways how to move. I think that Foucault is correct to say that discipline is a tool of authority and power when external standards such as fitness shove activities into injection molding to make Lego blocks of reps and sets. This disciplinary mold promises validation to the compliant, but it can't provide a sense of belonging.

Discipline is a beginner's readiness for transformation; it becomes organic, respecting and guiding how beginners actually move. Sinister disciplinary mandates are replaced by humbling task-specific challenges. Dedicated within and to some discipline, you have not become your own disciplinary dictator. Ironically, you gladly become more abjectly and utterly submissive to *transformation* than any dictator could ever command.

A mindset and culture of open-ended inactivity biases you against believing in and valuing your own *disciplined* capacities. This mindset and culture framework allows you to speak about the power, speed, and strength, *et al.* of wild animals and new automobiles, but not as your own capacities. When you think of discipline exclusively as external or internalized disciplinary authority, you create a false dilemma: you either indulge in personal practices (leisure as escape) or else conform to external disciplinary standards; you must either remain at the children's table with personal tastes and private indulgences, or else grow up at the price of conformity to external authoritative standards. What's missing from this false dilemma is the option of exercising your own capacities, individually or collectively, in meaningful ways.

If you are at a point in life when authority figures loom large, you may experience this dilemma as a bad choice between submitting to authority or else doing things "your way." Sadly, "your way" seems to belong nowhere and has little purpose other than resisting authority. Owning your discipline can too easily be dismissed as internalized disciplinary authority. And you don't challenge the authority of discipline by internalizing it. You only make its authority all the more insidious and secure. The dilemma clips your wings, because flying is either trivialized or else assimilated to authority. Disciplined activity as personal, autonomous, intentional, competent, deeply social and community-building practice is not the disciplinary structure of parents, schools, factories, and armies. It's your belonging in the world.

3. Paradoxically, discipline as commitment to and capacity for qualitative change isolates you from your surroundings so that you may belong anew.

It sounds like a paradox, but disciplined activity is something deliberate, committed, and sustained which isolates you from everything else around you and which at the same time allows you to belong more completely. This is not exactly the isolation of solitude. This is the selective devotion and commitment that learning and practicing any skill requires. You renew and sustain that special isolation across time and against a background of other motives, interests, necessities, and competing concerns.

You Always Belonged and You Always Will

Whatever your age, abilities, or place in life, there are no substitutes for your own animal activity. Don't adopt the Victorian bias that your animality is brutal, beastly, and beneath your humanity. Efficacious activity is the very best of your animality and is completely worth your time and sweat. Applaud and affirm this animality in others because this belonging is a transferable grace. If you're unsure about what this means, attend a marathon or a Special Olympics.

That isolating discipline is irksome but buoyant; supportive but restrictive; confining yet liberating. A discipline is different than a pastime, because it means committing yourself and not merely keeping busy or killing time. Your discipline's distinctive isolation can simultaneously be a deeper and more abiding belonging as you create concourse. You can miss this if you associate discipline only with resolve, hard work, and punishment. It's true that resolve is the usual down payment for discipline, but if resolve were enough, people would transform their lives every New Year's Day. Besides, you don't belong because you resolve to belong. You already belong (and you always did).

In the 25 meditations, I claimed that belonging is not earned. Belonging is not a reward for hard work though it's often treated that way. We seek confirmation of our belonging from others, but belonging is your readiness to change, not an external perk to work for. You know that meaningless work is alienating, so the solution appears to be "meaningful work." By now, you should smell a rat.

In fact, this sounds like getting off the couch and exercising as an alternative to inactivity. Meaning-enrichment is not belonging, and why expect labor to produce belonging along with income, goods, and services? 18th century philosopher John Locke[10] argued that people own their own bodies and make something their property through their labor. A workaholic does not labor to belong, even if he does not know how to belong anywhere else. The most pernicious job alienation is ceasing to believe in your own capacities. Whatever belonging you experience on the job or elsewhere means "owning" those capacities or enabling others to do so. That's how discipline nurtures belonging.

This is why discipline is different than punishment though both may feel like unpleasant burdens. We often think of discipline as externally imposed correction and suffering perhaps because there's something authoritarian about discipline, even, or especially, when you make yourself do something. However, even when developing discipline is painful, it confers a distinctive ownership. That is one difference between being subjected to discipline as correction or punishment, and developing a discipline through practice and training.

Therefore, it's not a paradox that the selective devotion of disciplined activity isolates you from much outside its boundaries while enabling you to better belong wherever you live. We feel belonging as we move with strength, or control our speed, or endure without exhaustion. Your various disciplines enable you to make *concourses*, even as they set you apart from other interests, activities, and competing concerns. Foucault was right to claim that disciplinary authorities and institutions use disciplinary compliance to exercise social control. Meaningful skilled movement must acknowledge this if it's going to carry any interpersonal social and political credibility.

However, if we view discipline exclusively as social control, we risk misrepresenting discipline as nothing more than a power game. Discipline of any sort must find or make personal and social meaning long enough, and hang onto meaning resiliently enough, for you to learn, practice, and exercise your capacities. Yes, authoritarian control often masquerades as mundane discipline and normality. But you don't prevail by abandoning discipline to go "your own way." You prevail by spotting manipulative counterfeits which exploit your need for a sense of belonging in your activities. You belong as you own your disciplines and experience belonging while you live.

At their best, disciplines are more engaged than the busiest schedule and more experiential than special events. Disciplines are *engaged* because they require mindfulness about the world and not just being busy with the world. Disciplines are *experiential* because they cannot be developed through practice and training without risking failure. The stakes are higher power and speed because they invest the other skills. Metaphorically, one makes an empty place and reserves empty time in ones' life to develop a discipline. The western idea of 'discipline' started in monastic communities. Vows of poverty, abstinence, or obedience sound like recipes for emptiness, yet monks sought a kind of belonging not only in their communities but within their disciplines.

Perhaps I've convinced you that "discipline" is not always grim or dirty. Its intimidating and authoritative connotations remain because discipline is so damn useful for social and political control. Sometimes we add self-discipline to the mix to sustain motivation and drive. Should I have chosen a word with less baggage as we explore belonging? I stick with "discipline" even if you think it's a self-imposed dead weight or socially-imposed burden with no place in the heart of belonging. Why? Because you should rescue those horses you've thrown overboard. Reclaim your capacities: wind power, wind speed, wind strength – and all the rest. Notwithstanding those inactivity doldrums where no one really belongs, you can make discipline sparkle from the inside out. Perhaps you'll make a new one! And you may even enable love, truth, justice, peace, and courage to belong in your activities.

If you're still oppressed by the pervasive authoritative power of imposed controlling discipline, reject *resistance vs. submission* as a false dilemma. You have a third meaningful and powerful alternative. Consider very carefully, and perhaps for the first time ever, that single most secure, reliably abiding, and compelling authority already in your possession. This authority trumps every competing claim to legitimacy. Unlike other authority perched atop disciplinary mandates, yours needs no such foundation. You need only gratefully accept my blessing from the living to the living: *You belong.* That's all the authority you need. You belong, therefore your life matters.

PART TWO

COURAGE, JUSTICE, PEACE, TRUTH, AND LOVE

CHAPTER 6
Power and Speed Belonging with Courage

Which demands more courage: belonging or *not* belonging? Both present risks, don't they? To get a new feel for courage, I invite you to rethink how you experience power and speed. In *Courage: The Politics of Life and Limb*, Richard Avramenko defines courage as "risking life and limb for the sake of a fundamental value." His definition of courage doesn't explain which values are fundamental, or which risks count for courage. But let's begin with your kinesthetic mix of power and speed. These capacities aren't just about transforming environments. Power and speed also leave you open and vulnerable to transformation. Otherwise, what's the point of courage?

1. **Power is not a resource but a capacity to invest other capacities. Courage means doing so with the constraints of speed.**

2. **Power to make a difference is not the same thing as force. Power is presumptive and uncertain until tested.**

3. **Because you apply power with force, force and power are easily conflated. However, power invests capacities to make a difference. Force, particularly as destruction and violence, risks little or nothing. Force has no power to transform.**

4. **To make a difference in the world, it is not enough to reclaim power. You must also reclaim speed. You then have the capacity to not only transform the world, but to become transformed. You become courageous.**

**

1. Power is not a resource but a capacity to invest other capacities. Courage means doing so with the constraints of speed.

Before you think of courage first and foremost as a virtue or imagine brave heroes, I invite you to think of courage itself as *using power and speed to risk yourself and your capacities.* Power applies force to make a difference. It is striving because power transforms internal and external environments. Unexpectedly, speed is more about belonging than striving. That may seem counter-intuitive since we think of speed as belonging nowhere for very long. However, speed isn't necessarily about moving fast. It's your capacity to control rate and tempo of movement. Your capacity for speed is about more than acceleration.

I know that speed seems the antithesis of belonging. But start running and you'll quickly remember how speed makes you vulnerable to qualitative time-sensitive change. If you think that belonging means staying in one place, you might miss this. Belonging, after all, is knowing what to do with yourself. As you make speed, control your speed, and experience speed in activity, you meet, if not match, your environment's temporal terms of engagement: duration, tempo, timing, rhythm, acceleration, or plodding.

Power and Speed Belonging with Courage

Even a runner striving to cover more ground wants thereby to belong on new terms. Otherwise, moving faster or slower wouldn't matter.

It's my estimate that courage is about 80% power and 20% speed; courage is mostly striving but slightly about belonging as well. If you think that ratio is too timid, try 90% power and 10% belonging. Striving makes things possible, belonging makes them matter, and this lopsided ratio hovers in the background when people personally or collectively muster courage or judge someone's actions to be courageous. By risking vulnerability to transformation, people can disproportionately transform quite a bit of their environment.

Commentaries going back to Boethius' *Consolations of Philosophy* remind us how the powerful always fall prey to new dangers. Being subject to Lady Philosophy's turning wheel of fortune is common to all. But courage is not common. The deeply conservative inertia of power is to preserve itself rather than risk itself to make real change and become something new. Don't pretend that power is only about kings and billionaires. Every time you apply force to make a difference, you use power, whether opening a stuck jar lid, jumping over a puddle or defending yourself.

Physics, mechanics, and the technology of energy production create the impression that power exists isolated as an impersonal reservoir to tap. That makes it easy to suppose that power is water behind a dam or lodged in a battery. Think instead of power not as force (or stupendous quantities of force) but as force applied to make real change. Taoist teachings on the power of the weak and yielding come to mind. If you think of power without context and as a "thing in itself," it's no longer a capacity to respect or invest.

In fact, power can become addictive because power as a "thing in itself" has no borders or boundaries. One never seems to have enough, whether it's energy or influence. Place your power instead within the context of your speed, strength, flexibility, and endurance, *et al.* and that power becomes humanized, if not entirely humbled, as one capacity among others. Power is then revealed as your own gamble. You act powerfully as you invest your other capacities, combining and focusing them to make a difference.

Instead of channeling, hoarding, or distributing some "thing in itself" called power, you might wager your own strength and flexibility in the short term. Your investment of capacities may be long-term, summoning your endurance and stamina. When the gamble risks your own life and limb for the sake of transforming the world, you muster courage. In the eyes of others, you have become a different person, set apart. Courage is born.

So, when does exercising power count as acting bravely? Your risk must be personal (you risk yourself). "Making a difference" means justifying the risk for the sake of some fundamental value. We have spoken of transformation in this way. Speed is your capacity to act at a rate which best enables a real difference. Mix speed and power in the wrong ratio, and your gamble might work but be dismissed as foolhardy and heedless. Courage is no engineering ratio, but I believe that your sense or aesthetic intuition of that lopsided ratio between striving and belonging shapes how you muster and judge courage.

2. Power to make a difference is not the same thing as force. Power is presumptive and uncertain until tested.

I'm certainly not claiming that the complex interpersonal and institutional meanings of power reduce to physical capacities. The context of social and political power has evolved throughout history and involves concepts of authority, legitimacy, obedience, and domination. When you jump, climb, or push, that's vastly different than international politics except that, in both cases, *power remains uncertain until risked.*

Experience informs us about the scope of our capacities (insofar as they've developed). What experience cannot teach is whether gambling those capacities will work, and whether you have the capacity to gamble/invest them effectively. When we conflate the meaning of power with that of force, we suppose that a great deal of force means a great deal of power. In a political context, a presumably powerful country can fail unexpectedly in a minor test of power. Or a powerful country applies overwhelming force which makes no real change and transformation. Until power is risked, it remains presumptive and uncertain.

In Chapter 11, *The Politics of Transformation,* I explore this theme of testing power further and make the argument that, because each life belongs in every life, you need a politics of belonging before you have any trustworthy politics of borders. Otherwise, borders create violence and injustice instead of representing our reasonable expectations for each other. The use of force in disciplinary power is also considered, and I make a case that people do have the power and may find the courage to subordinate the disciplinary power of bias and coercive conformity to their transformative values. They can't end bias, but they can corner it and live a meaningful alternative.

Power in politics or in movement is risky and uncertain as it commits other capacities such as endurance, stamina, strength, and flexibility, to create change or ensure stability. Whether we're discussing politics or exercise science, the capacity we must stand upon is necessarily shaky. Be it ever so circular, power doesn't fully exist until tested, and that pathos of power plays out in how we admire, envy, fear, and resent power.

No matter what type of institutional power you favor, you may think that those in power do not deserve what they get from a gamble, particularly if they gamble with other people's lives. You resent the unilateral nature of power most when it's applied to you. Feeling most powerless, you'd much prefer a society which is interpersonal, reciprocal, principled, consensual, and which honors inter-subjective give and take. Even power humanized by other capacities unilaterally slashes across social contracts and relationships, and unilateral power doesn't share.

3. **Because you apply power with force, force and power are easily conflated. However, power invests capacities to make a**

difference. Force, particularly as destruction and violence, risks little or nothing. Force has no power to transform.

So far, we've considered power only as benign or neutral, and anyone painfully acquainted with the violent and destructive uses of power will accuse us of whitewashing all the ways that power dislocates lives and makes rubble of environments. Why on Earth should we expect belonging in the face of destructive power?

I'll do my best to address this with a story. Our philosophy department at Elon University once resided in a lovely old two-story wooden house on the corner which  had been the Colclough family residence for several generations. The house was demolished in June 2006 after our department relocated to a new building. The contents of the house were first distributed with appropriate respect for the former owners and consideration for the community's needs, but the quick and powerful demolition was deliberately an event with no ribbon-cutting, groundbreaking or public ceremony. In less than a day, our academic home became rubble. By silent consensus, bringing the power to destroy into public foreground and witnessing was deemed unseemly. A grassy lawn covers the site, graced by a work of public art. Even constructive power often means rationalizing destruction, so what does this mean for belonging where you live?

Watch a two-year old stomp an anthill flat and wonder *whether "applying force to make a difference"* is even remotely connected with a sense of belonging. Speedy destruction takes hubris but it doesn't muster courage. No fundamental value is affirmed. However, perhaps it's a mistake to blame power at all. Un-making tiny lives is not making a difference (or anything else). Imposing force is not applying power. It's force for the sake of force. I don't think "impose vs. apply" or "force vs. power" splits hairs. Unilateral force is quite different than unilateral power. The toddler's wanton destruction dramatically reduces the meaning of power to that of force. It makes power a proprietary entitlement to flaunt force and un-make. Young or old, people are unlikely to humanize power removed from its context of other movement skills. When nothing significant is risked or affirmed, when power needn't go begging to other skills for support, when failure is not a possibility, when no personal limits are encountered, the thrill is about applying force, not power to make a difference.

Notwithstanding, in a world of rapid and widespread destruction, belonging does have reason to hope. You can do more than clean up the debris. First, destruction means loss, and loss should be grieved, not dismissed, explained away, or cleaned up. In grieving, heart and lives are transformed by acknowledging the value of what's destroyed before making room for new belonging. Otherwise, new belonging reaps a shaky and precarious status sown by casual destruction. How mindfully we destroy, as much as whether we destroy, enables or undermines our future belonging.

Someone who uses a gun to commit violence does not want to be vulnerable in any sense. And the victim's surviving family friends, and community are made newly vulnerable to trauma and grief. I live in Durham, N.C. which has a high murder rate. The Religious Coalition for a Nonviolent Durham, Parents of Murdered Children (www.pomc.com), and Durham Congregations in Action respond to violence by sponsoring vigils against violence. When the family and friends of a homicide victim request such a vigil, a religious leader, supporters from the community, along with the survivors, gather as soon as possible with family and friends for that vigil *at the murder site.* The vigil is about endurance, to be sure, and a kind of strength. Its stamina is a commitment to bear witness.

Power is the application of force to make a difference. Participants in these vigils literally force themselves to gather at the terrible place so soon after the homicide, but they do so. It's a brave mix of power and speed. I've joined several of these Durham vigils, some in neighborhood cul-de-sacs, or across the street from McDonalds, and I can attest these are timely applications of force which make a difference. The chalk lines and yellow police tape have long since been taken away. At those places, we pray, bear witness to the person who was murdered, and, with solidarity of heart and spirit, commit that we – not the murder, not the killer, not the yellow police tape - belong where we live and that the victim belongs in our hearts and as a member of our community. That transforms us into people honoring the victim. We belong together especially to bear suffering but also to show that we will not be evicted from our lives or places by violence, loss, and grief. Those vigils also show us how people skillfully mobilize their strength, endurance, and flexibility in reaching out to each other.

4. **To make a difference in the world, it is not enough to reclaim power. You must also reclaim speed. You then have the capacity to not only transform the world, but to become transformed. You become courageous.**

The lopsided mix of power and speed matters for courage. Subtract speed, and you find that exercising power is no risky venture but only a nondescript capacity to do certain things, more things, or perhaps wonderful things, but not courageous things. What's missing is speed's sense of belonging It's hard to separate power from force in our emotional experience of living under both. It's hard to take risks or hope for transformative change when you are so relatively powerless that courage feels more like desperation and futility. But don't forget your speed.

I once visited a sanctuary for tigers. The student tour guide showed us fenced enclosures for tigers rescued from zoos, circuses, or other places where they had been mistreated or abandoned. This sanctuary provided these large cats with trained care,

much of it done by trained volunteers. The tigers had refuge, sanctuary, and asylum to live out their days with much more space than some room-sized metal enclosure with a concrete floor. It was not the miles of territory enjoyed by tigers in the wild, but each was at least 100 feet wide, surrounded by sturdy chain-link fence. If you wonder whether a tiger can ever "belong" anywhere but in the wild, you have opinions about animal rights or animal welfare, but I was convinced that the tigers belonged here on better terms of captivity than in the past.

The students and I gawked at tigers and walked up to one enclosure which was empty except for a box in one corner. The perplexed guide decided that a keeper had transferred the tiger to a different enclosure without telling her. As we resumed our tour, one very un-transferred tiger crouched down behind that box, waiting patiently for us to turn our heads. It then sprang to cover 100 feet in a few silent bounds and pounced with all its weight against the fence just inches behind us. We jumped and screamed! Had we not experienced the tiger's silent speed, we wouldn't really understand how it belonged there, perhaps stalking visitors to relieve its boredom or playfully practicing a kill. Again, belonging is less about place than movement possibilities.

Like power, speed affords a distinctive satisfaction. We can feel it vicariously through motor vehicles. But controlling your speed feels different than having speed imposed upon you. We experience contemporary life as  a diffuse pervasive pressure to adapt to an accelerating tempo. Our conversational "speed-speak" mimics how we once chatted about weather. *"It seems there are just not enough hours in the day. Can you believe the season is half over? Where did all the time go?"* Speed has been externalized and out-sourced to technology and society; essentially to no one in particular. Therefore, challenging this speedup is as futile as trying to change the weather. You may feel that your only alternative is to grouse, drag your feet, or pin your hopes on some blessed oasis of "time out." Even when speed increases to the point that most Wall Street transactions happen in nanoseconds, we speed-speak that the world is moving faster all the time, always has been, and that we can only try to keep up.

In Chapter 5, *Rethinking Discipline*, I explored Foucault's distinction between a disciplinary society and a disciplined society. Speed-speak is one version of the disciplinary society in which discipline is the tool of power and control. It fosters the same kind of false dilemma: either you indulge your trivial personal "time out" or else submit to an external discipline. The meaningful alternative of owning your speed goes unacknowledged. Learning, practicing, nurturing, and enabling a sense of time and speed appropriate to honoring our capacity for speed must be intentionally sustained by a community. Otherwise the false dilemma forces a choice between dropping out or else submitting to a hectic culture of busyness. There's no time for meaningful change because no one can claim to own the speed.

One sad effect of externalizing speed is losing ownership of social reform and progress. Once speed and tempo is accorded a life of its own *unrelated to your activity or that of your community,* you'll hear speed-speak nostrums such as "reform takes its own time", or "meaningful change is slower than you'd like, but there's really nothing anyone can do about that." Speed-speak honors the truth that good and worthwhile things can take a long time but says nothing about time-sensitivities of social reform and progress which demand speed. For belonging, the point of speed isn't whether you run fast or walk slowly. The point is to develop your own skillful speed which helps your community to better belong with the rate of time-sensitive opportunities and possibilities of your environment. Speed can be exciting, exhilarating, and empowering, but also satisfying, gentle, and decisive. Best of all, it's *your* speed!

In *Godspeed: Racing is my Religion* (Continuum, 2009), L.D. Russell considers that perfect storm of popular culture and big business which is NASCAR racing. Notwithstanding all the jibes against NASCAR as a low-brow spectacle in which race cars make circles as fast as possible, Russell does not overlook its most basic appeal: drivers risk life and limb for the fundamental value of victory. In short, it takes *courage* to compete in such a race. On a grand scale, power is thereby anchored in speed and yields (in the judgment of many) a display of gladiatorial courage.

Your prolonged inactivity in a fast-moving vehicle is probably a somewhat different experience, to put it mildly. Don't hope to experience belonging, much less glory, sitting in a car. Not surprisingly, you feel belonging nowhere in transit nor with drivers around you. When you actually move your arms, legs, and body in walking or running, you experience speed differently. It's not just that you produce the locomotion.

You must call upon your other movement skills. This is speed with self-imposed limits and trade-offs but with a greater sense of belonging. Do you want to get over a 4-foot high wall? You could slow down and climb over it, or sprint and vault over it. Either way, you leave speed-speak behind. The daily aggravation of imposed speed needn't rob you or your community of the delight and benefit of owning speed. When the "pace of life" (a pace that is weirdly unrelated to your particular life) threatens to make peacefully belonging anywhere impossible, don't lose hope. Decide for yourself the rate of living at which you want to think, feel, love, and respond to the word, or do so as a community. Let that be your "local time."

At some level you already know that "life is getting faster and faster" is ultimately an insane and unsustainable picture of life. Be especially suspicious when this nostrum justifies some status quo at your expense. If the first casualty of war is truth, the first casualties of imposed speed are your questions, hesitation, reflection, ability to change course, and speed-ownership. Who has time for belonging or courage? As a child, I remember an adult telling me poignantly that "when the band starts playing, people start marching." You and your community can belong where you live and act with courage as needed without marching music.

We often think of emergencies as settings for courage, and you may be called upon to respond quickly to some disaster. If you "apply force to make a difference" despite fear and for some value greater than yourself, you may act with courage. But just what is an emergency? You might name top contenders such as hurricanes, floods, earthquakes, and medical crises, but think instead about the very idea of an emergency. It is some infrequent, brief, but grave event which disrupts normal activity and puts safety and wellbeing at risk. These disruptive events demand speedy response, and failure to respond rapidly puts victims at more risk. That's speed and power, perhaps graced by courage, but within a passion play of rescue and recovery.

However, not all dangerous situations count as emergencies. Dangerous situations may happen chronically, intermittently, or last for indefinite stretches of time. It's hard to call a protracted, widespread, rapidly changing or ill-defined danger an "emergency." That doesn't make the situation harmless or inconsequential, but we're not hard-wired or culturally prepared to mobilize power and speed on those terms. Chronic illnesses which ravage health may have periods of remission and flare-up which defy emergency fixes or medical cures. You and your community have a "fight, flight, or freeze" response to crisis calling forth rescue, intervention, and supererogatory exertion which you can't sustain indefinitely. As that dangerous situation drags on, you and your community may not know quite how to summon power and speed to deal with one crisis after another. The word "emergency" no longer serves as you adapt by tuning out those crises just as people now ignore strangers' car alarms.

If you need a political slogan try this: *There is no substitute for belonging where you live.* The people don't just need power. They need to reclaim speed as well. Perhaps you see many forms of non-political power open to you, but are uncertain about the possible rate of change. The key question is not "How fast can you transform your environment?," but "Are you now ready for real change?" That's vulnerability to transformation. Think of power only as potency bestowed or an asset in your personal account, and you miss transformation which is better than any destructive revolution. Fail to own your speed, and you subtract belonging from power. Belonging then becomes trivial personal attachment; power becomes impersonal, external, and manipulative.

Speed likewise becomes an external taskmaster determining the tempo of your change and activities. *Courage? Who has the time for courage?* Whether you're an Olympic weight lifter, confined to a wheelchair, or recovering from hip surgery, you do have the capacity to apply force to make a timely difference. Power is not for king of the hill. Forget kings and hills for a moment and consider that there is no substitute for feeling that you belong where you live, individually or as a community. If you're ready for this change, you have the speed to claim the time. You have the power to make a difference, whatever your capacities.

Climate change is good closing topic for considering ownership of power and speed. People have traditionally answered the power and speed of hurricanes and floods by summoning their power and speed. Public urgings to fight climate change attempt to summon that power and speed, but climate change is no temporary disruption. Climate was once our stable and abiding frame and background for life's business as usual, but now worldwide meteorological imbalances seem a never-ending emergency affecting everyone though not at the same time nor in the same ways.

So, can we justify continuing to call climate change an "emergency?" We hope to have a normal life after an emergency, but this "emergency" promises no "after." Here too, there is no substitute for belonging where you live. Whether that takes a multitude of situational adaptations and improvisations, mutual aid on a global scale, an overarching climate policy which is both effective and timely, or all of these things, people who own their speed and power are less likely to feel helpless and more likely to be of help to others. Perhaps that's whom we'll look to when all the creeks are rising and our courage needs bolstering.

CHAPTER 7
Strength and Flexibility
The Reach of Justice Against Resistance

Strength is physically experienced as the ability of muscular units to apply force. It's your ability to kick, grip, lift, carry, pull, or push things.
Flexibility is experienced as stretching and contracting muscles within a range of movement around a

joint. Strength, like power, seems such a positive value in virtually any context that even strong smells, strong misgivings, strong temptations, and strong villains get concessive nods.

A child imagines a hero with strength to vanquish foes and surmount obstacles. But when adults isolate and idealize otherwise salvific strength, it becomes brutal and fascist, abandoning rescue to dismiss anything or anyone deemed weak and powerless. It seems that only strong animals belong in those tiresome wildlife documentaries, invariably narrated in a deep male voice, featuring pouncing predators. These films so blatantly pander to male domination fantasies that I call them "pred-porn." This is strength gone very, very bad, and this is not the best place to find justice.

However, flexibility goes bad too when we isolate and abstract this capacity away from how we experience it in movement, and make flexibility into an open-ended value. With no anchoring and stabilizing joint, and unfettered by any optimal range, it's easy to believe that flexibility can be stretched to the point of Gumby-like elasticity, moving in any direction while affixed no place in particular. The scope of justice doesn't feel that way. When we speak of extending the range of justice, we mean that people who have not experienced it before might now do so.

Flexibility can mean bending the law without breaking it and is the span within which we proportionately meet and surmount resistance. When you think about the scope of rules and principles in justice, imagine them as joints dictating a span of movement. The neck joint has a different range of movement than the wrist. If we have never tested that range and try to do so, we experience pain, frustration, and failure. Let's not conclude that the principle is too rigid. Perhaps we ourselves are rigid. The problem may not be that the principle is too good or too ideal to put into practice but that we've forgotten that, like flexibility, justice tends to improve with practice.

I invite you to consider four claims about the kinesthetic "feel" of justice:

1. **Strength and flexibility together afford a primal experience of proportionate equity, just so, and the right amount of reach against resistance.**

2. **Strength and weakness can be re-imagined as integral to our experience of justice rather than as problems for justice.**

3. Your experience of flexibility provides kinesthetic intuition about the reach of justice and fairness.

4. The optimal relationship between strength and flexibility is embodied in the peace circle.

**

1. Strength and flexibility together afford a primal experience of proportionate equity, just so, and the right amount of reach against resistance.

Let's humanize strength and flexibility within the interactive context of your other capacities. You naturally stretch muscles through resistance, so strength partners with flexibility to become hybrid "strexability." Strength humbly supports endurance and agility, sustains balance and coordination, and submits to being risked in power and speed. This is strength as a capacity in relationship with other capacities, not strength merely full of itself and nothing else.

Those gory film tributes to leaping leopards and pouncing panthers gratify viewers' predatory fantasies by hiding the truth that predation often means going hungry or being injured by a prey fighting for its life. Other predators may steal your prey, for real strength is played out within vulnerability to loss and privation. Strength is not a private asset to deploy, but a muscular relationship with need. It is a way of belonging in the world. Contracting against resistance, muscles move things (including oneself). What was at rest is put into motion. Flexibility, on the other hand, strives to stretch, to turn, and to reach.

With strength, you might move to secure and keep contact. *"Hang on!"* and *"Don't lose your grip!"* invoke strength. Think of a rock climber who secures and keeps a grip by contracting muscles against resistance. Could muscular strength be a basic experience of equity? We think of equity as interpersonal comparison, perhaps between "haves" and "have nots." Strength, as contraction against resistance within the scope of flexibility, provides force equal to and appropriate to fairness.

At the risk of stating a truism, how you feel when your strength does not merely match but surmounts resistance, is a kinesthetic experience of proportionality and equity. That experience of "what works," "the right amount" or "just so" in strength's give-and-take interaction with the world gives justice weight and direction. I'm not reducing weighty matters of justice to the mechanics of movement.

I'm inviting you instead to ask a new question. Instead of assuming that justice will always encounter resistance from human nature or vested interests, ask: *why should justice encounter resistance at all?* Think of resistance not in terms of moral negatives but as strength's distinctive vulnerability. If we experienced no such vulnerability when acting in strength we would literally "not know our own strength." Strength only belongs when exercised against resistance.

You might then be less inclined to treat strength as unilateral force by remembering that you experience strength against resistance and in the context of a specific task and together with your other capacities. Unlike comic book super-powers, real strength is no essence or magic applied to the world. Developing and exercising strength for the sake of justice means that you can respond appropriately to resistance. Whether you're climbing, pushing, pulling, lifting, gripping, or advocating, your strength abides in ongoing give-and-take with your surroundings. Further, you give something up for the sake of cultivating and sustaining this relationship.

1. **Strength and weakness can be re-imagined as integral to our experience of justice rather than as problems for justice.**

If you think of "strexability" as a way to experience equity, you don't thereby make equity merely subjective nor do you reduce justice to muscle twitches. The ways in which you bear weight lend intuitive conviction that responsibility means shouldered weight. If you quote the New Testament (or Spiderman[11]) to declare: "*With great strength comes great responsibility,*" don't forget great weakness! One casualty of isolating and glorifying strength is that moral responsibilities associated with relative weakness are dismissed and not taken seriously. The weak bear weight at greater cost. So, proclaim with equal conviction: "*With great weakness comes even greater responsibility.*"

Weakness in movement demands being all the more keenly and intentionally aware of your relationships with surroundings and the possible consequences of actions, particularly for others. We may call it "disability" relative to some able-bodied norm, but this heightened awareness of limitations summons more mindfulness and initiative than exercising strength. Strength and weakness are simply different responses to resistance, and you exercise neither by remaining inactive. Each is response-ability to take limits and possibilities seriously. Likewise, you may exert force against your own movement in self-restraint. Although it sounds metaphysically convoluted, we intuit that forbearance forcefully resists our own impulses. That is strength.

So, should the strong lift great burdens while the weak lift little or nothing? The question commits the fallacy of treating strength as an isolated asset and commits the bigger fallacy of defining obligations in terms of our own capacities. You wouldn't make a duty out of unconditional weight-bearing, unless you're Atlas.

Think of weight-bearing as an animal's dispositional way of moving in the world – a kind of "pre-duty."[12] A pre-duty means that, strong or weak, you're already moving weight and bearing weight. This kinesthetic shouldering relationship with the world supports (pun intended) the prospective credibility of more specific obligations to persons, places, and the life around us, but doesn't choose them. "Strength" by itself (individually or communally) doesn't specify how much weight should be born. "Weakness" is not exemption. Otherwise Spiderman's swinging strength would make his stories boring and predictable, and those deemed weak would be left with bitterness, resentment, and no clear belonging with substantial ethical responsibility. [13]

On a recent visit to Berlin, I visited Brandenburg Gate (*Brandenburger Tor*). That gate has many different meanings for German history and Berlin in particular. King Friedrich Wilhelm II and architect Carl Gotthard Langhans, who built the Gate in 1791, wanted the gate to symbolize strength through peace. The statue of Nike /Victoria is strong enough to hold the reins of the four horse quadriga in one hand while holding aloft an oak wreath of peace. At least that was the original intention. The oak wreath has since been replaced by swastika and then iron cross. Strength as end in itself can be more compelling than strength through peace. But the mighty Doric columns remain. I noticed a small kiosk on the edge of those columns. Since 1994, a group of volunteers from a variety of religious organizations, have sponsored and sustained this small enclosed chamber for peace and silent meditation. It contains no religious symbol. No matter what the Gate comes to symbolize, this group was determined that people might experience belonging in peace and renew their strength only a few feet away from the noisy plaza on *Unter den Linden.*

2. Your experience of flexibility provides kinesthetic intuition about the scope of justice and fairness.

When a group culture glorifies strength, flexibility is usually demeaned. Strength gets star billing in fitness culture while flexibility has a minor supporting "warm-up" role. Outside the context of yoga or Taoist wisdom about the strength of bending like a reed in the wind, flexibility faces biases that strength matters more than flexibility (as if these are competing options), that the strong needn't be flexible, and that flexibility is only for the weak who bend only because they must. Better coaches know better. If only to minimize injury or speed  recovery from injury, coaches treat flexibility as a kind of movement flossing - good hygiene for strength training. Without flexibility, bending and stretching in any direction becomes difficult, hazardous, or simply impossible. Strength is then confined to ever-smaller spans of movement and exercised just long enough to injure oneself. Painful movement in yoga means unwise movement choices. In wrestling, it can mean stretching past the point of pain, but not to the point of injury.

You find a more lopsided dynamic of strength and flexibility in theories of jurisprudence and social expectations for justice. When justice and law are extolled in their resistance to anarchy, corruption, and self-interest, this appeal to strength accommodates flexibility only in the margins as caveats and judicial discretion. When people cry for justice, they want strength, not flexibility. So, let's examine our intuitions about fairness in terms of flexibility.

Flexibility makes a poor first impression. Before you can increase muscles' span of movement at a joint, while stabilizing the joint, bone, and ligaments, you endure discomfort. Flexibility's first message is "You can't do this." Neglect to develop flexibility, and you can expect the same message with each infrequent stretch. Try to extend justice beyond its customary reach, and expect howling. Try this only occasionally and it feels "above and beyond" and you thereby "prove" that increasing the reach of justice is a bad idea.

By contrast, within yoga, flexibility is the star attraction. Moving particular joints and muscles through a range of movement complements controlled breathing and are integral to developing overall balance as well as strength. Our culture of protracted inactivity makes flexibility look like supererogatory achievement. An unexpected demand for fairness becomes "a stretch" given our lack of flexibility. If your experience of flexibility is mainly acute discomfort and failure, can you confidently distinguish integrity from rigidity?

Strength and Flexibility ...

When you need to bend the rules without breaking them, what flexibility experience informs your judgment? It's not so much a matter of becoming more flexible (or stronger), but lacking a feel for flexibility as one capacity among others. Without that "feel," it's harder to know what counts as flexibility: an ability to change (your mind, your loyalties, or your position), accommodating opposition, adaptation to stress, or making useful and necessary compromises, or just giving in.

Like strength, flexibility is humanized within the context of our other capacities. It is not an isolated power to bend on demand. There's no flexibility in muscles at a joint without some history of stretching muscles and ligaments at that joint. Therefore, we can't solicit flexibility like battery power. Without that history, flexibility does not come readily or easily. For this reason, inflexibility and flexibility are not evenly distributed among all joints and muscles. None of us twists freely in every direction like Gumby. Developing flexibility in major joints can improve balance and harmony for the entire body, but not before one has invested time and stretched beyond initial discomfort in developing flexibility.

Likewise, you aren't equally flexible in all directions. Gumby is elastic, but not flexible. Flexibility is capacity for movement relative to a fixed joint, and muscles and ligaments can't stretch without attachment to stable joints. You might guestimate your flexibility span relative to joint-equivalents such as non-negotiable rights, fundamental principles, and values. However, we also treat our prejudices as joints. We try to move around them, and we bumble, stumble, and otherwise move without grace. Identify your real joints. Otherwise, you are trying to move relative to your biases. Passive-aggressive elasticity *("I don't really care. Whatever you say is fine with me.")* isn't flexibility. It avoids conflict but it does not make fairness.

You are not flexible in the same ways at all joints. Flexibility does not occur *however* we wish to bend. What's the range of movement? For physical flexibility, that's partially determined by the type of joint and connective tissue. For example, the ball and socket shoulder joint has greater range of movement than wrist or ankle joints. You lessen resistance of connective tissue without damaging it. Flexibility can be practiced socially and politically with movement around a particular "joint" but less so around another. For example, you may need to reduce resistance of certain social bonds to increase flexibility, but without damaging or breaking those bonds.

Like strength, flexibility is interwoven with our emotions. The mind associates (and the body remembers) unresolved negative feelings with stiffness and inflexibility. In knots of tightness, muscles do cling to emotional habits and memories. Past injuries can limit present flexibility. In contrast, we associate pleasure with ease and flow of movement. Either way, flexibility, like strength, is a capacity we misunderstand and out-source in a culture of protracted inactivity.

3. **The optimal relationship between strength and flexibility is embodied in the peace circle.**

It may still be hard for you to think of justice in kinesthetic terms of strength and flexibility. Jails prohibit mobility and courtrooms minimize movement as a matter of decorum. A jurisdiction's sentencing grid seems as far removed from muscular exertion as the Periodic Table of Elements. However, the peace circle is an ancient way of making justice which beautifully embodies kinesthetic intuitions about conflict and fairness.

The peace circle is a kind of contraction against resistance, but flexible enough to expand to admit new members or address new conflicts. A "peace circle" elegantly illustrates justice experienced in communal contraction, expansion, and closure. The peace circle is also a consensual and egalitarian form of communal weight-bearing. The format is simple enough for children to learn and practice, but the circle can be strong enough to bear massive adult conflict, heavy trauma, and oppressive power confrontation. Kay Pranis[14] has done much to revive and re-introduce this ancient format into contemporary conflict resolution. Though she specifically credits the Tagish-Glingit Nation and Yukon Territories as longstanding practitioners of the circle, the format is global though marginalized by top-down state-imposed forms of justice.

Ms. Pranis has brought the peace circle to modern institutions and mediation conferences. Ironically, she most successfully introduced peace circles to resolve staff conflicts within a state prison. "Flexibility" is not the first word that comes to mind for that venue. However, combine it with strength and you create a dynamic for fairness and conflict resolution. The participants voluntarily arrange themselves into a circle facing each other with no (physical) obstacles separating them. To do so, they exercise strength to resist the inertia to remain apart and in conflict. They choose a meaningful centerpiece for the circle, and they select a talking piece ("peace pipe") which each participant passes to his or her neighbor.

The person who holds the talking piece may speak without interruption, and all participants have agreed to listen carefully. One participant is keeper of the circle. The circle-keeper establishes the meaning of the format, clarifies the values and rules agreed upon by participants for the circle (the joints), and guides it towards resolution. Combining strength and flexibility, the peace circle "strexably" allows participants to reach resolution and experience belonging. Participants in the circle make decisions by consensus, and all circle members agree to abide by guidelines (flexibility around joints) established by the group based on shared values, in order to work toward a common goal. That is the circle's political character.[15] Spiritually, it is a form of sacred space where people come together with their strengths and weaknesses.

The circle participants may have very different economic, social, cultural, or political backgrounds. They may be of different ages. The circle is flexible enough to accommodate and strong enough to support them all. However, the participants' willingness to intentionally commit to practice and abide by certain values in the circle (e.g. mutual respect in how one speaks and listens, and honoring compassion) to exercise strength through getting acquainted, gathering perspectives, telling stories, making a decision, healing trauma, or even sentencing an inmate, bears weight whether the circle has six members or a hundred.

For indigenous people, the peace circle's center was important not just as an equidistant point, but as a stabilizing focus. Different tribes often used water. Life naturally gathers around a watering hole. Water symbolizes cleansing, renewal, purity, and belonging in the world. People find themselves in living environments forming communities around water, literally or figuratively.[16] As a spiritual ceremony, as a format for conflict resolution, as a way for neighbors to share their stories, keeping the circle is a discipline of individual and communal strength with flexibility equal to the task. Through the circle, participants reach far enough to make and sustain contact, lift burdens, grip difficult feelings and issues, and release themselves from isolation.

I urge you to resist the temptation to reduce your capacities for strength and flexibility to muscular movement. This is not figurative speech. Participants in the peace circle do not "figuratively" exercise strength and flexibility. Nor do they bring opponents into negotiation and reconciliation "as though" or "as if" they exerted strength and flexibility. They exercise strength and flexibility as genuinely and literally as they might in yoga or weight training.

For example, coordination, which we will consider in the next chapter, is a transferable skill. Develop one form of coordination and you find coordination easier elsewhere in "unrelated" contexts. So, take the bypass around mind/body dualism to appreciate that strength and flexibility are no less literal and substantial when exercised socially and politically than in acrobatics. Don't underestimate the range and power of your movement capacities while stuck in a culture which thinks meaningful activity is unlikely and unrealistic. Nor am I making an analogy, claiming that the reach of justice is like touching your toes. I claim that our intuitive confidence about bending without breaking comes from how we move in the world.

The Platonic allure of justice as an ideal Form or *thing in itself* is very strong. And thinking of justice as strength against resistance relative to real joints instead of fake ones (biases), doesn't address partiality and impartiality. I deal with impartiality more in Chapter 9 – *Agility and Accuracy – Truth be Nimble, Truth be Quick*, but if impartiality is essential to not just to the reach of justice, but as part of its essence or fabric, I am clearly on the wrong track. You may also think of justice in aesthetic terms of harmony, balance, and symmetry. Chapter 8- *Balance and Coordination: Matched Partners for Peace* may interest you more. I argue that impartiality and equality are experienced in truth and peace more than in justice. The Platonic idea of justice treats it as isolated from those values rather than one capacity in collaboration with others.

Meanwhile, I invite you to consider that your capacities of strength, partnered with flexibility, inform your expectations for how justice "works" or even whether it can work. Remain asleep in the nightmare of non-belonging, and righteous anger about injustice becomes resentment and grousing. In dreamland, there's nothing substantial to resist nor is there specific scope for activity. In that bad dream, justice and transformation remain out of reach. *Why bother? What can one person do? You're just wasting effort!* As you awaken, stretch your muscles and feel their proportionate resistance. You can reach out and join hands in a circle too.

CHAPTER 8
Balance and Coordination Moving in Peace

In the Introduction, I described peace as "50% belonging and 50% striving" to express the idea that, personally and politically, peace is equal parts balance and coor- 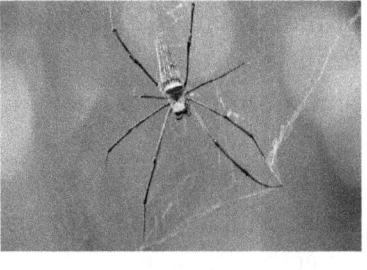 dination. You experience balance as ability to control placement of your body's center of gravity in relation to its support base. You experience coordination as you combine several distinct movement patterns into

Balance and Coordination Moving in Peace

a singular distinct movement. Put them together, and you get a remarkably dynamic way of thinking about peace. You or your community live "at peace" when your belonging matches the scope of your striving. In other words, your sense of balance keeps pace with how you coordinate activity.

Balance in movement is a form of belonging because it's openness to qualitative change: you land on your feet or fall down. You move in relationship with your base of support. Treat balance as a static or precarious arrangement, and you fear that outside change will rock the boat or disturb your peace. Likewise as you coordinate individual movement patterns into a whole, you strive. Whether your coordination shows great mindfulness and dexterity or automatic ease, its intentionality, control, and sense of movement-as-relatedness reduces fragmentation, futility, wasted effort, interference, and feeling out of place. You strive to move in sync.

The 50/50 description also conveys the idea that peace, unlike courage or justice, is a value which lacks a vector. Its striving does not exceed belonging, so you experience presence more than directionality in peace. Belonging does not anchor striving as it does for courage and justice, but instead embraces striving and gives it a home. In short, peace is not "going anywhere." It doesn't need to. It need only abide to legitimize both striving and rest.

Theologian Frederick Buechner describes this match between striving and belonging as a kind of spiritual just-rightness. One is at peace when your need matches the world's need:

'The kind of work God usually calls you to is the kind of work (a) that you need to do and (b) that the world most needs to have done...the place God calls you to is the place where your deep gladness and world's deep hunger meet.'5

This is not peace experienced only as quiet or nonviolence. It is not merely the absence or cessation of warfare. This is peace felt as *shalom* or *salaam* in which life can stand upright with hope of becoming whole and complete. Balance and coordination are transferable skills across very different contexts. Imagine young hikers crossing a stream together by stepping from one slippery rock to another without stumbling. That's not a bad model for peace activists. So, don't dismiss balance and coordination as metaphor without political relevance or consequence. Imagine (or remember) the panicky feel of losing your balance or feeling betrayed by your body when you stumble and flail about, unable to coordinate your movements. Lose trust in your balance and coordination, and you won't risk activity (or activism) at all. Isn't that how it feels to be a community robbed of peace or unable to find peace?

I will borrow a phrase from comparative planetology to describe what I mean by the absence of peace. This is "chaotic terrain." Such topography, whether on Mars, Mercury, or Europa, can't be appropriately described as mountains, valleys, deserts, or plains, because earthbound landscape words falsify these expanses. Chaotic terrain is utterly without clear borders or integrative pattern, often the jagged aftermath of cosmic collisions and eruptions, frozen in time. Politically, warfare is an intensely destructive patch of chaotic terrain, but war is only one patch in such an expanse. A person trying to walk through this alien terrain would find it impassable – labyrinths with no clear entrance or exit, or endless ridges and rills with no orienting landmarks. Survey the terrain and you see no prospects for movement.

Likewise, when you survey your personal or political terrain, you may not see peace anywhere. Therefore, I invite you to turn from that chaotic terrain and look instead to your own disciplined capacities to balance and coordinate. I want to argue for these four claims about balance, coordination, and your experience of peace:

1. Coordinating activity with balance, relative to a base of support, builds confidence in peace. Treating peace as an external process of balance and coordination makes balance seem precarious, makes coordination appear tentative, and makes peace appear unsustainable.

2. Peace is less about place, equilibrium, and harmony than about movement confidence. Movement is our ongoing choice to risk losing and regaining place. Place is springboard, place is landing spot, and making a way is also making place. Animals are at peace as surely and reliably in motion as in any favored place.

3. Personal peace and emotional balance is not about opposition, counterweights and counter-forces, but how well you endure vertigo while striving with hope.

4. Peace is coordination, balanced with respect to a base of support, not to manipulate and control, but to weave movement into a meaningful whole. Balance on the move hospitably invites such coordinated activity.

**

1. **Coordinating activity with balance, relative to a base of support, builds confidence in peace. Treating peace as an external process of balance and coordination makes balance seem precarious, makes coordination appear tentative, and makes peace appear unsustainable.**

Balancing in your activities is different than fidgeting to get proportional symmetry and equal amounts, as in bookkeeping. *You feel balance as movement-confidence.* You can't isolate this experience from your ongoing relationship with gravity by reducing "balance" to "equilibrium" among interdependent parts of a self-contained system maintained by feedback. That describes internal homeostatic equilibrium beset by imbalances. But feeling imbalance is different than losing your balance. Imbalance undermines equilibrium while losing sense of balance undermines confidence about stepping out into the world.

Imbalances are varied: fever slows you down, and imbalanced brain chemistry leaves you depressed or anxious. You or your body responds by correcting internal deficiencies or excesses. But balance experienced while walking is much different. You lose and regain balance with every step. That's not perpetual incompetence. With confidence, you trust loss and recapture of balance, and this iterative risk-rhythm is a kind of belonging. When that trust falters, you find yourself "out of step," "out of sync," and fumble or stumble to recapture it.

If this is too much philosophical hair-splitting, take a break and answer a riddle: *Why does no balanced diet make room for chocolate and ibuprofen even though we consume them to correct imbalances?* You point out that a balanced diet is about proportions of food types,  and that chocolate and ibuprofen aren't food. But the diet is about balance in what I consume. Chocolate and ibuprofen correct imbalances, easing pain and improving mood. "Balance" isn't optimal proportions of foods, but an ongoing realignment of tastes and needs. Likewise, peace is not preserved by balance of interests, balance of needs, or balance of power. Peace does not totter until political equilibrium is found. Peace is robust enough to thrive on the move, through difficulties and in satisfactory balances.

What "balance" means for balanced budgets, balanced diets, balanced lives, balance of nature, and balance of power is *not* the balance you feel positioning your body in motion relative to your base of support. These system equilibriums don't capture balance as future-oriented trust to lose and regain equilibrium. Of course, you need both equilibrium and a sense of balance to walk. They're interdependent. But, unlike equilibrium, balanced movement never really gets "finished" even when a task is accomplished. In the same way, peace is not homeostatic tranquility. Politically and personally, peace means trusting in activity's future prospects.

2. **Peace is less about place, equilibrium, and harmony than about movement-confidence. Movement is our ongoing choice to risk losing and regaining place. Place is springboard, place is landing spot, and making a way is also making place. Animals are at peace as surely and reliably in motion as in any favored place.**

"A centipede was happy quite, until a toad in fun,
  Said, "Pray, which leg comes after which?"

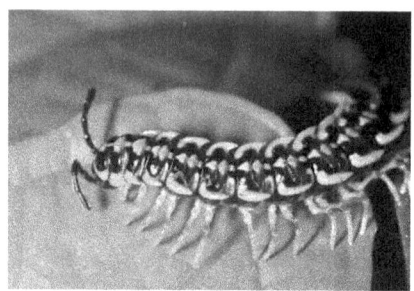

This raised his doubts to such a pitch,
He fell distracted in the ditch,
Not knowing how to run."

-Mrs. Edmund Craster (1871)[17]

It's a paradox. You keep your balance by losing your place. Politically, this paradox is quite different than trying to secure peace by ensuring a place for everyone. We are an ambulatory and migratory species, so it's strange that people on the move are treated as problematic simply because they lack place: dislocated and relocated, transient and in transit, refugees and illegals. We belong as firmly and reliably in motion as in any place, and you change place and location without thereby sacrificing peace (or falling into a ditch). You recover equilibrium by finding and correcting imbalances (make an audit or fight an invasive species). However, when an animal loses balance, movement becomes hesitant and unsure. We blame violence for snatching peace away, but what's lost is a community's movement-confidence.

Before we problematize place rather than movement in belonging, let's acknowledge belonging as emotional attachment to, or fierce defense of, spot, turf, territory, and home. What exactly is the place of place for belonging? Philosopher Edward Casey suggests as a thought experiment that we try to imagine *atopia*: a world without places. It's virtually impossible because to exist is to have a place. Yet animals are mobile and therefore must surmount this challenge of ongoing displacement as a way of life. Casey notes:

"Animal life refuses the immobility of the plant. Animals, including human animals, are not only able to change their places, they must do so if they are to survive. No given place suffices indefinitely...Human beings are among the most mobile of animals. We are beings of the between always on the move between places... Getting out of place is therefore a basic action of all animal, including human, life. But with the freedom to change places...comes the danger of getting lost. A plant, having no place to go, is never lost. A mobile animal, however, continually confronts the unhappy prospect of disorientation of not knowing its way between places...The home territory embodies the plenitude that being placeless so painfully lacks." [18]

Plants have many tropisms of their own, and perhaps a plant tricked into blooming in the wrong season experiences, on its own stressful terms, being "out of place." However, Casey reminds us that *animals repeatedly surrender and reclaim place through movement.* Thriving plants spread out, animals move plant seeds and spores, but plants don't surrender or choose place. They move, or are moved, to take root.

They may belong in habitats, but migrating birds, upside-down tree sloths, and dolphin pods in the open sea also belong in distinctive movement. Movement isn't a crisis. They don't suffer existential malaise from iterative surrender of place and quest for place. Place is not irrelevant to belonging, but neither is place *definitive* for belonging. Whether there's no place like home or you're at home wherever you go, being receptive and vulnerable to transformation is what matters for belonging. If a place protects you from change, that very security steals your belonging. If your role protects you from change (being a tourist), you belong nowhere.

3. **Personal peace and emotional balance is not about opposition, counterweights and counter-forces, but how well you endure vertigo while striving with hope.**

What's worth losing your balance? Falling in love, good fights, and roller coasters are disturbers of the peace if you think of personal peace as comfortable equilibrium. Take a vacation from equilibrium to renew trust in your sense of balance. You may not get that balance back right away, but you and your balance will find each other eventually. Count on it.

Balance and Coordination Moving in Peace

Consider that some "imbalances" don't need balancing. Peacemakers may not trust former enemies or survivors of war and persecution to resume life's activities in peace. But a traumatized post-war society (or an antisocial teenager) may have a hidden gyroscope or the functional equivalent for self-correcting orientation and stability, testing coordination and seeking balance. If you think of peace as real insofar as it is "lasting," remember that building peace is also learning to keep ones balance in movement without stumbling or bumping into others. That can take awhile. Sometimes peace reveals itself only in a split-second so it looks perpetually jeopardized when it's not really wobbling at all. Don't despair. And don't blink. Peace is at hand.

Is peace something formidable or fragile? Balance and coordination mix both ways. Boston Dynamics has invented a wonderful teaching aid for formidable peace.  The company has developed an all-terrain quadruped robot, "Big Dog," to accompany soldiers. Big Dog is more mule than dog, but it combines balanced and coordinated quadruped movement for all terrains and this peacekeeper is downright creepy. Practically no collision knocks Big Dog off its "feet." In stark contrast, consider the gentle balance and coordination of flower arranging. Your aesthetics of equilibrium may lead you to arrange flowers for a quick symmetrical and finished display. If you practice Japanese *kado*, you cultivate asymmetrical balance, artful unevenness, and incompleteness, suggestive of life and movement. In peace, as in movement, balance is ongoing, open-ended, and unfinished.

In western thought, Newton's third law of motion that mutual forces of action and reaction between two bodies are equal, opposite, and collinear influences what we expect from peace. Seeking an equilibrant – a single force which balances the effect of one or more other forces - can hold peace hostage. We needn't assume that balance is necessarily about opposition. Counterbalance has a more ancient pedigree in Eastern thought. The Taoist idea of two opposite forces is not a story of mutual cancellation, but about forces interconnected and interdependent. Newton's law doesn't explain where the forces come from, but yin and yang, as characterized in Lao-Tzu's teachings are opposite forces which generate each other. Yin and yang exist only in relationship with each other. In contrast, two forces described by Newton's laws can exist independently. Remember that balance experienced in peace isn't a feud between dualities but rather a trustworthy relationship with ones base of support.

Likewise, problems of emotional equilibrium are rarely fixed by finding counter-balance. Negative feelings aren't canceled or balanced by positive ones. For example, the loss of someone significant is like losing your sense of balance for you feel unable to resume motion and direction. You feel that you're moving "on automatic." How do you find peace in the aftermath of serious loss? Belonging is vulnerability to qualitative change, and grief qualifies. This capacity for transformation is not canceled nor do you restore balance by cheering up or thinking positively. Significantly, good advice about emotional balance invariably recommends some discipline of skillful interpersonal activity such as being both assertive and cooperative. Recovery is, in part, relearning day by day what to do with yourself.

People can feel awkward in the company of someone who has just suffered serious loss. Perhaps they try to be the counterweight, which is silly, but we intuit the need for something hefty even when no words seem to have enough weight. A leader in Stephen Ministry once recommended saying: *"I'm very sad that this happened to you."* Give your own sorrow a home in the relationship and thereby make a place for the griever's sorrow. That's enough balance for belonging.

4. **Peace is coordination, balanced with respect to a base of support, not to manipulate and control, but to weave movement into a meaningful whole. Balance on the move hospitably invites such coordinated activity.**

In sports, dance, and everyday activity, coordination is a multi-layered sequence of blended movements, building to performance at greater speed in a constantly changing environment. The pleasure of coordinated movement is not just about manipulation and control (efficacy), but enjoyment of flow, unity, and grace of crisscrossed patterns of response and adaptation. This is not just fumble-free activity. It is part of what living in peace feels like. Replace peace with ongoing stress, and multi-tasking is the best you can hope for. Like coordination, multi-tasking keeps two or more activities from interfering with each other (more or less), but can't blend activities. When peace is only a memory or hope, that blend vanishes and seems impossible. Activities no longer know how to blend or you are afraid to risk blending them.

For peace, coordination needs to equal balance: in leadership, management, choreography, team performance, foreign policy, emergency response, or forming group consensus. When coordination lurches ahead of balance, people with the same needs and wants can be clumsy at satisfying them; thoughtless, counter-productive, and confrontational for no good reason. Coordinated movement is less "command and control" than practiced habits and improvisations which build, adjust, and re-adjust patterns of movement which are embraced (and spared dizziness) by a commensurate sense of balance.

Those patterns may be incredibly complex, but they're not for that reason incredibly fragile. Those coordinated patterns flow not just without obstruction, but flow despite obstruction. They intersect, perhaps in tension or outright conflict, but thereby add to each other's meaning constituting a whole greater than the sum of its parts. Sometimes, people "get it together" individually or in community when coordination is needed quickly and unexpectedly, as in an emergency.

"Evolutionary biology awaits an extended discussion of what an 'individual' is. Who counts as an individual seems obvious when thinking of ourselves, our pets, livestock, or other organisms who become detached from their parents. But individuality is not

so clear-cut in other species. A grove of poplar trees consists of many trunks springing from one seed – what is the individual, a single tree trunk or the entire grove?"

– Joan Roughgarden, *The Genial Gene: Deconstructing Darwiniam Selfishness*(2009)

The example of the honeybee reminds us that balanced and coordinated activities exist simultaneously on many levels. Humans have made themselves totally dependent upon bees for our crops while making it hard for bees to belong. Bees reproduce individually through mating and collectively as a swarming hermaphrodite super-organism. Bees coordinate movement most impressively as a colony.[19] They vibrate to maintain a constant temperature in the hive, respond collectively to danger, organize reproduction, care diligently for their young, and they do this all through coordinated movement of thousands of individuals. There is no "command and control" structure. The queen bee makes thousands of eggs, but the colony brings together countless movements into an intelligent super-organism.

Balance and Coordination Moving in Peace

Perhaps for this reason, humans (particularly beekeepers) have a different emotional relationship with bees than with other insects. You may worry about getting stung, or be fascinated with the inner workings of the hive, but I believe that what we experience in (safe) proximity to a swarm is peace. It's not peace in the sense of tranquility, but rather a dynamic exchange between balance and coordination in which there's not a single fatal collision. The individual insects may qualify as "busy bees," but the swarm is a presence.

Humans do not particularly shine in large groups, so our envy is understandable. But we shine in our own way: think about what happens when you and a stranger walk toward each other. One must move to the right or left to allow the other to pass without collision. That can be accomplished in different ways such that the encounter expresses good will and hospitality. Of course, it can also convey deference or contempt. Hospitality makes and shares place with another. You coordinate your space and resources to meet another's need for shelter and safety. The stranger responds appropriately by taking on the role of guest with gratitude. The 18th century philosopher Immanuel Kant thought that hospitality was a necessary part of any culture:

"Hospitality means the right of a stranger not to be treated as an enemy when he arrives in the land

of another. One may refuse to receive him when this can be done without causing his destruction; but, so long as he peacefully occupies his place, one may not treat him with hostility. It is not the right to be a permanent visitor that one may demand. A special beneficent agreement would be needed in order to give an outsider a right to become a fellow inhabitant for a certain length of time. It is only a right of temporary sojourn, a right to associate, which all men have. They have it by virtue of their common possession of the surface of the earth, where, as a globe, they cannot infinitely disperse and hence must finally tolerate the presence of each other. Originally, no one had more right than another to a particular part of the earth." – <u>Perpetual Peace: A Philosophical Sketch</u> by Immanuel Kant (1795)

This is coordinating your movements, space, place, and home with the needs and value of another. In *Perpetual Peace*, Kant grounded the human right to receive hospitality in our common possession of the earth's surface. Unfortunately, in the 18th century, "common possession" meant "common" among humans only. It certainly did not include honeybees. It was "common" only for humans lucky to have enough power and status to count as persons. Imagine how history would have changed if Amerindians and Europeans followed Kant's sane advice on how to treat each other!

Balance and Coordination Moving in Peace

The earth's biosphere, with its thin veneer of atmosphere, is finite, especially under pressures of overpopulation and environmental degradation, so we might agree with Kant, for reasons of our own, that scarce space on the surface of the Earth dictates entitlement to place - not only for hosts and guests, but for all life on Earth. *Peace* on Earth requires more than a secure place, however. Peace means coordinated satisfaction of needs, wants, and goals without sacrificing anyone's relationship to a base of support. Neglect balance, and you find that even life which is not in conflict or danger will nevertheless feel threatened and disconnected. Neglect coordination, and even the most balanced budgets and diets won't meet anyone's needs. The partnership of balance and coordination is dynamic. The turf may be finite, but there is no reason for peace itself to be scarce or fragile. Animals experience peace and provide peace in distinctive ways, and if we don't see much peace in human affairs, perhaps we're not looking in the right places. It's hard to appreciate the bee swarm when you're worried about getting stung.

CHAPTER 9
Agility and Accuracy
Truth be Nimble, Truth be Quick

What is truth? You already have compelling intuitions about how truth feels. If your intuitions feel less so, blame our culture of busy inactivity with its "accessing" framework of banal risk-free exploration. I invite you to consider the ways in which you combine your capacities for agility and accuracy to shape your exploratory expectations for truth. Are these intellectual capacities or physical ones?

For our purposes, it doesn't really matter. Before you sort claims into dualistic categories such as "subjective or "objective;" before debates about whether truth is the value of propositions, or embodied in art and lives, or just our current collective consensus about what we take seriously; before you throw up your hands and despair of ever finding truth, know that you do have a good kinesthetic feel for truth. It may less sharp and honed than it might be, but consider these four claims:

1. **You experience truth by striving for accuracy with enough agility to change position and direction as required by that truth.**

2. **We need both accuracy and ability to experience truth in our activities. Without agility, accuracy becomes pointless precision. Without accuracy, agility is only reactive shuffling and not a response to truth.**

3. **Agility is a moving response to a truth's requirements in which truth-seeker, quest, and the world change position and direction.**

4. Agility and Accuracy combine to allow us to experience the truth of a crisis in which "doing the right thing" is likewise an experience of truth.

**

1. You experience truth by striving for accuracy with enough agility to change position and direction as required by that truth.

Philosophers discuss truth but seldom consider whether (or how) people move, and I think this oversight shortchanges the interactive dynamic of truth. For example, think of objectivity not as knowledge free of all subjective bias (good luck on that), but as expecting *what you know* to discipline *how you can know it*. The conditions under which truth may be encountered then dictate best approaches to that truth. That approach summons your agility. Your intentional vulnerability to those "truth conditions" allows you to nimbly approach truth.

At the risk of repeating myself, this capacity, like the others, is unavailable when you're inactive. Inactivity makes you more likely to expect truth to arrive and present itself on your terms. Armchair philosophers discuss truth, test concepts of truth, and question the meaning of truth. But these tasks are different than getting yourself in a position to feel and test truth, whether it's truth of heart or truth about a larger world.

Perhaps you're much too skeptical about prospects for *getting it rig*ht, *hitting the mark*, or *ringing true* to entertain my claim that you have any credible intuitions about truth. Perhaps you think I'm now trespassing on philosophy of mind and should go back to the gym where muscular capacities belong. You may believe that truth is too complex, too ambitious, or too problematic a value to grip with mere muscular capacities. All the same, I hope to convince you otherwise. Agility is how you belong in a changing world as you strive to accurately hit the mark. What is that ability if not a kind of broken field running towards truth?

You're agile when you effectively change the direction and position of your body without loss of speed, balance, or body control. Agility is currently a popular buzzword for business pundits: agile teams, agile corporate response to changing

markets, agile programming, and agile customer service. But you don't find many images of corporate agility or even human agility with your web browser. You'll see plenty of dog shows and the occasional athlete doing ladder drills. Like power and speed, agility has lost its currency as an everyday way of engaging the world. Agility has been out-sourced to athletes, externalized as a corporate virtue, and attributed to Airedales. Don't bother jumping over any candlestick, because no one expects you to be agile.

What about accuracy? We describe approximations for the sake of truth as a quest for accuracy, but accuracy is not an end in itself nor is accuracy about greater precision in how we represent the world. Accuracy isn't an arrow which hits the target. The arrow and target find each other by taking on the roles of "arrow" and "target." In our experience of truth (not our criteria for truth), accuracy is not about copying the world, but changing direction or position quickly and appropriately to match a truth's requirements. Precision is not accuracy. In the words of Henri Matisse, *"L'exactitude n'est pas la verité."* A wrong answer or a false statement can be impressively precise, but inaccurate.

What about agility? This capacity is one way that you manage to belong in a changing world.

Otherwise, you experience that change as distressing, overwhelming, and exhausting. No sooner do you master one pattern than it becomes irrelevant to what's needed. When your world is turned upside down, truth does not call for a paradigm shift, but rather ability to land adroitly on your feet. That sudden unexpected event which calls for agility may be fun or it may be a crisis. Either way, you risk missing the truth if you don't move accordingly.

We don't think of fumbling as truth-error, but you've no doubt experienced the anguish of having the right words, or the truth "slip through your fingers" even as you clutch it. Still, we describe commitment to truth in terms of honesty and curiosity, but rarely as agility. If it makes you feel any better, theologians don't often credit God with agility. Aside from the occasional pious accolade for spiritual timeliness, prevenient "just rightness," or adroit providence, God is not expected to be nimble. Apparently, if you're omnipotent, agility is somewhat unseemly.

The experience of truth in activity is not stoic detachment (perhaps a euphemism for inactivity), but instead moving in such-and-such a way and doing that now rather than later. Agility is not about being impervious to shocks, sudden turns, upsets, or calamities. It's your capacity to remain upright while accurately abiding with truth, notwithstanding sudden changes in position, direction, and orientation.

2. **We need both accuracy and ability to experience truth in our activities. Without agility, accuracy becomes pointless precision. Without accuracy, agility is only reactive shuffling and not a response to truth.**

Precise movement can be beautiful, and an insatiable demand for detail, completion, totality, or exactitude can be useful and desirable (in the right contexts) for discovering and honoring the truth. This is accuracy at its striving best. Accuracy communicates that 'this matters' or 'this is worth superordinate control and care' or 'this matters enough to measure, count, or assess diligently.'

If you idealize truth as ultimate accuracy (for which neither you nor the truth belong anywhere in particular) you've only picked a target and called it "truth." Truth combines accuracy and agility. Accuracy without agility becomes silly, painfully limiting, or irrelevant to the truth. What do you say to someone who replies to your invitation to go for a walk, hang out, chat, or make love, with the question 'What's exactly the point of this?' 'What's this precisely supposed to accomplish?' or 'How much longer is this going to take?' When accuracy does not partner with nimble accommodation, we dismiss it as obsession, compulsion, and pettiness. Exactitude notwithstanding, someone has missed the point.

Notwithstanding, accuracy sometimes not only moves us closer to truth, but we aspire to truth in the disciplined exercise of this capacity. Traditional Japanese aesthetics of harmony and simplicity in the tea ceremony, calligraphy, and martial arts (*wabi-sabi*) elevate patterns of accurate movement and timing to art and a way of life requiring years of discipline. Accuracy in transcribing a sacred text, assembling computer circuits, performing neurosurgery, or making any quick but smooth transition is accuracy's grip on time and place. Agility in dodging or feinting sometimes matters in a fight more than power, speed, or strength. Moving with accuracy and agility honors the time and place specificity of truth.

3. **Agility is a moving response to a truth's requirements in which truth-seeker, quest, and the world change position and direction.**

Timing is your sense of when something should be done. With timing, you move with a sense of the propitious moment. If you're merely specific about time and place without showing much accuracy or agility, you may get points for punctuality but not necessarily for being where you belong. Without the timing of agility, you can arrive at exactly the time and place you promised, but still too late or too early. You're on target, but in the wrong place. Accuracy conveys that "this matters" or "this is worth superordinate control and care" or "this matters enough for me to be nowhere else but at the right place time." Aristotle's account of doing the right thing sounds like an appeal to accuracy: *"[To] do this to the right person, to the right extent, at the right time, with the right motive, and in the right way, that is not for everyone nor is it easy; wherefore goodness is both rare and laudable and noble."* [20]

Right action, whether in the framework of Aristotle's Ethics or Buddha's Eightfold Path aspires to accuracy as a way of life. When your way of life, whether right action, right speech, right effort, or right intention, manages to hit the mark, that existential accuracy inspires others to trust you. Sometimes doing the right thing is time-and-place sensitive. Think of accuracy achieved with agility as a down payment on trust. Accurate movement and doing what's necessary to be in the right place at the right time can communicate care, respect, and even compassion. On the other hand, small inaccuracies or casual inertia can sow skepticism about your credibility.

Suppose that you conceive of truth as your goal. That picture of truth has plenty of problems, but, if you imagine running towards that goal, you assume that the starting block and finish line are fixed as you run between them. What if you, the finish line, *and* the starting block are all in motion? The shortest distance to the truth might not be a straight line. The Hohmann transfer orbit is a good example of this three-body problem. In 1925, engineer Walter Hohmann calculated the most efficient (least time and energy required) elliptical transfer orbit between two objects orbiting in the same plane. Think of a spacecraft traveling from Earth to Mars. The spacecraft would not move in a continuous straight line to Mars. A particular ellipse is quickest and most direct route.

Assume that a genuine truth (whatever is your best candidate for abiding and time-tested truth) remains stationary as you approach it. In the alternative, assume that you're stationary as the truth (experienced as grim but unavoidable certainty) looms closer. Either assumption might lead you to miss the truth. Consider how you might move between your moving assumption and a truth which likewise moves. Discover how to nimbly and accurately dwell in these movements, whether traveling to Mars or getting at the truth of a situation, consider that truth might be somewhat less about accuracy than agility. My hunch is 40% accuracy and  60% agility. If you can't go home again, and your truth has moved, don't panic. Move accordingly.

For example, if fiction contains brilliant truth, does its accuracy matter? On the other hand, what brilliant truth *doesn't* deserve accuracy? Whether you think accuracy is essential or optional for understanding a truth, your care for accuracy and your readiness to move as that truth dictates does make a difference. Truth can be a wonderful interplay of departure, journey, and destination, difficult to represent, but you can still know how it feels. You may not wind up where you intended or expected, but when your capacities for accuracy and agility join forces, *here and now* stand a better chance of becoming the right time and place for encountering truth.

Here's the paradox of discipline again. Truth-seeking is a discipline subject to different criteria and prospects, depending on the context. But the quest isolates the seeker from his or her mundane context without for that reason making the truth (or the truth-seeker) sacred. Figuring out truth is intelligent, caring, and persistent and frustrating practice through a series of inaccurate and not-yet-nimble moves. This discipline can be isolating and demanding, but your "feel" for truth in activity confers new freedom and engagement. It makes hitting the mark and good timing less a matter of luck. Yes, the voice of discipline has an authoritarian disciplinary tone [21] which is not endearing. But sustained disciplined movement does not just trump fallacies and bully falsehoods. It's outward-looking and makes possible those changes which are only available through activity. So, this quest isn't really about self-discipline or disciplining others. [22]

A nimble dancer adapts to choreography just as an agile team athlete adapts to a changed offensive or defensive strategy. But the greatest agility is rapid and effective response to unexpected change and allows one to improvise in unexpected ways. Sometimes this is exactly what experiencing truth requires.

Also, we haven't considered the thrill of accuracy or the delight, excitement, and beauty of agility. Whether you're dancing, dodging around orange cones, hopping between rungs of a ladder in drills, or adroitly responding to a debate rebuttal, you're practicing – and *enjoying* – agility. Agility is a very tactile satisfaction about how we engage the world.

In our culture, we confuse agility with the multi-tasking ability to hop back and forth between projects and venues. Sometimes multi-tasking encounters a bottleneck, or one task interferes with another, resulting in errors and slower performance. Multi-tasking metaphors such as juggling and surfing are about rapid surface attachment and detachment. But broken field running is a better metaphor for agility. Agility requires actual commitment to some direction or position. Agility is not about doing one thing at a time, but doing one thing gracefully and smoothly, despite transitions and obstacles.

4. **Agility and Accuracy combine to allow us to experience the truth of a crisis in which "doing the right thing" is likewise an experience of truth.**

If your world is figuratively turned upside down, the challenge may not be doing many things at once, but rather landing on your feet. The sudden and unexpected event may be fun or it might be a crisis. You might welcome the unexpected as novelty or dread being forced to quickly change your direction and position to satisfy an authority or deadline.

Agility and Accuracy Truth be Nimble, Truth be Quick

We have lower accuracy and agility expectations for public institutions, even at their best, than for individuals. Leviathan manages to move but can't hop or tapdance, and when institutions face a crisis, this limitation can be painfully apparent. Unprepared and traumatized institutions respond clumsily to abrupt changes in a society's direction or position. Likewise, people robbed of community try to recover enough agility to transition from war, natural disasters, and political oppression to normalcy if freedom, rescue, and relief are at hand. Transition is not just instability but also a period of stumbles, clumsiness; slow and uncertain responses. It's not just first responders who prize accurate assessment of needs and agile response in a crisis. Those in need want and expect these capacities. Accuracy and agility honor the truth of a crisis or emergency.

Without agility, people are still standing, like earthquake survivors, but uncertain about where or how to move when all is rubble and aftershocks are possible. After a crisis, people don't yet know what to do with themselves, and the world doesn't quite know how to handle or heal these people except to give them aid, along with generic, gratuitous, and decidedly distancing labels: *that flood of refugees, the growing unemployed, chronic homeless*, and my tectonic favorite, *victims of social upheaval*. At best, institutions shift gears slowly. How agile are you when you're faced with a crisis? What about the groups you belong to? Have you ever had to find out?

Here's a story about institutional agility:

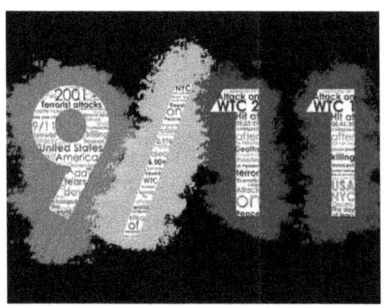

"On September 11, 2001, St. Paul's Chapel escaped destruction when the World Trade Center buildings collapsed across the street. Although the churchyard and church were filled with debris and dust, there was no physical damage to the building. From September 2001 to May 2002, St. Paul's Chapel opened its doors to firefighters, construction workers, police officers, and others for meals, beds, counseling, and prayer. Medical personnel, massage therapists, chiropractors, podiatrists, and musicians transformed the chapel into a place of peace, rest, and reconciliation." [23]

It's an inspiring story in many ways, but it's also an example of not just charity and volunteerism, but service *agility*. Agility can be the grace to transition quickly and effectively into new patterns to meet needs. A priest from St. Paul's Chapel told me that emergency personnel didn't wait for the church to open their doors to provide refuge and assistance on 9/11. *They broke the lock and forced their way in.* Nonprofits try to hone better-than-average institutional agility to respond to unpredicted and sudden needs to transition from crisis to safety.

We are grateful when we can respond with agility, and we're likewise thankful when others help with enough agility to meet unexpected and urgent needs. Thankfulness is interesting – it's our response to the blessing "you belong." You can feel deep gratitude for agile assistance (a better description than "rapid response") even without knowing who or what to thank.[24] When we don't have enough agility to help people in crisis, we feel overwhelmed.

It's unfair to blame those who tax our agility. It's even worse when blaming justifies estrangement from those who need help.[25] If agility is just for those who are fit and have lots of energy and security to fall back on, then the old, sick, and poor have only themselves to blame for their inadequate response to change. They become not just victims of crisis, but hapless, clueless, burdensome victims who don't know what to do with themselves. That's not the truth of a changing situation. Together, rescuers and rescued nimbly change their positions and directions in response to the truth conditions, striving to accurately assess needs and resources. That's a shared commitment to truth as well as compassion.

CHAPTER 10
Endurance and Stamina Love's Suffering and Hope

It's no surprise to find love in a book about belonging, especially a book insisting that each life belongs in every life, and that every life belongs in each life. What  value is more intimately associated with belonging than love? Before you judge whether love endures, consider first how you experience endurance itself. Search within affection, obsession, devotion, and heartbreak, and you find dogged endurance and stamina giving credibility and currency to all these expressions of love; perhaps not at first try, but keep searching. I will argue that these two capacities are where we learn that love matters and that love can endure. Consider: How much would you believe in giving if you experience only giving in, giving out, or giving up?

Are the mystery and otherness of spiritual encounter "places" where the living can ever hope to belong? That depends on what you think of communion or belonging with God. Spiritual disciplines for such encounter can forge compassionate relationships or promote solitary inner contemplation. Spiritually, "discipline" means making disciples. In a military corps, discipline is a core social value.

Gaia's sheer scale challenges our comprehension enough to mystify, even as Gaia *theory* tries to scientifically explain the mystery's workings. The quest to be situated in the scheme of things, whether seeking the purpose

of life, a destiny, or meaning, is, in part, a hunt for belonging. What makes nirvana, heaven, or paradise compelling is not just promised perfection of some sort, but the promise of homecoming and belonging. We have mentioned respect and compassion as part of belonging, but what about love?

In *Belonging to the Universe* (1992), David Steindl-Rast interprets Christian belonging in terms of love:

For us God's saving power is manifest in the religious experience, the experience of limitless belonging. In our peak moments we experience 'saving power' rescuing us, bringing us out of that which is most foreign to this sense of belonging, namely, alienation. The experience that we belong is the basis for Jesus' preaching of the Kingdom, expressed in contemporary terms. Then, the primary reference was to the community of the chosen people. But for us it is more broadly the experience of belonging and its social consequences."[26]

He raises the stakes with this affirmation: *"Love is saying yes to belonging. That's my definition of love, pure and simple. Anything that we call love, as far as I can see, is in some way related to this yes... And that saying yes is not just an intellectual assent; it has profound moral implications."*[27] I do not think that our self-sufficient Gaian framework prepares us for limitless belonging. What could count as preparation? In Chapter 13 – *To Boldly Belong*, I consider what the biosphere actually means for life belonging.

In Chapter 5 – *Rethinking Discipline,* I argued that operating in virtual domains requires skills, but the domains do not build spiritual or military discipline, prayer chains and war games notwithstanding. There are numerous sites and blogs dedicated to spiritual topics, but they are not sacred spaces or holy places. Without dismissing the potential of virtual connectivity, virtual reality can be full of surprises and even revelations, but it is deliberately and digitally void of mystery and ambiguity.[28] Cyber-warfare is real, but it does not flow from military discipline. Chapter 12 – *Virtual Belonging* deals with this further, but the existential point to remember here is that belonging means vulnerability to transformation.

As I discuss love and belonging, check my claims against your own experiences. Think not just about feelings of love, but your experience of love's *credibility*. That is, what has (or might have) convinced you to believe in love? Bring to mind personal trials which sorely tested your endurance and stamina. Although "resilience" has become popular to describe positive responses to stress, I stick with "endurance" and "stamina" because "resilience" is mostly about remaining intact and functioning despite stress. I am interested in an ethos for transformation, and resilience alone neither transforms nor invites transformation. Here are four propositions about how the capacity for endurance and stamina shape our confidence in love:

1. **Endurance is about your relationship with suffering, and stamina is about your relationship with energy. Trusting love and believing in love are the result of how we find and assign meaning to endurance and stamina.**

2. **As you summon meaning for endurance and stamina, you increasingly belong with suffering; this is a transferable capacity for love in which directionality risks suffering.**

3. **When you idealize endurance and stamina for peak experience or excellence, you strive but fail to belong with suffering. Likewise, when you idealize love for romance or a good cause, you strive but fail to belong with suffering.**

4. **Because endurance and stamina demand meaning, as does love, the most**

serious problem for these capacities is neither exhaustion nor opposition, but disillusionment.

**

1. Endurance is about your relationship with suffering, and stamina is about your relationship with energy. Trusting love and believing in love are the result of how we find and assign meaning to endurance and stamina.

Though we use "endurance" and "stamina" interchangeably to mean protracted vigor, endurance is ability to withstand hardship, whereas stamina summons energy to follow through. Endurance stretches resources while stamina discovers and seizes them. Thinking of sexual love in these terms is not exactly irrelevant to love but misses the point that lovers do not aspire to be endured and hope to mean more to each other than a finish line.

Whether it's passion or long-term care and devotion, love can motivate great endurance and stamina. For the sake of love, you summon both, yet endurance and stamina are not about human relationships. Endurance is relationship with suffering whereas stamina is relationship with energy. More precisely, endurance is how you belong with suffering, and that requires figuring out suffering's meaning. Likewise, stamina strives with hope, and that too drives us to find meaning and not just energy. Your other capacities such as balance, strength, or speed do not cry out in this way for interpretation. They don't send us searching for meaning.

I've argued that your capacities for power, speed, strength, flexibility, balance, coordination, agility, and accuracy combine to give distinctive feels to courage, justice, peace, and truth as part of your activities. This provides kinesthetic and dynamic conviction about values available only through activity. In the right circumstances, our animal capacities provide experiences of values which we nevertheless describe as ideal and transcendent. Those non-experiential descriptions may keep us from seeing how we experience those values in our active capacities.

However, endurance and stamina do not simply point to values. They are also self-referential. You experience not only hardship, but also *the person you become* as you endure with stamina. Your history of endurance and stamina then is not a medical chart. It's an ongoing personal testimony to what you become as you persevere. Even if your culture doesn't care about endurance and stamina and neither do you, I believe that these capacities drive you to find meaning as you belong with suffering. That same quest is also integral to experiencing – and risking - love. Belonging is vulnerability to qualitative change or transformation, and this is true for endurance.

Love isn't about how much endurance and stamina you have. I am not simply arguing that, without endurance, people can't sustain loving relationships which take time and impose hardship or that, if you overestimate or under-estimate your ability to withstand hardship, you misjudge your ability to help, defend, bear witness, collaborate, or otherwise love. That's probably true, but it's not my point. I am arguing that trusting love and believing in love are the result of how we find or assign meaning to endurance and stamina.

The most obvious objection to this claim is that people credit their past experiences of loving and being loved for enabling them to trust love. Likewise, they credit experiences of betrayal and abuse for never trusting love again. In many ways, love flourishes in the absence of suffering, and certain kinds of suffering such as betrayal make it hard to trust love. But, even at its sweetest and luckiest, love necessarily risks suffering and assigns meaning to it: this is the same capacity which you exercise in endurance and stamina.

2. As you summon meaning for endurance and stamina, you increasingly belong with suffering; this is a transferable capacity for love in which directionality risks suffering.

Like love, endurance is not a fixed static resource waiting in the pantry when needed. Faced with open-ended hardship, you ponder, interpret, and judge the prospects and meaning of the situation and the ultimate value of your endurance. *How long can you endure? Is this challenge worth enduring? What (if anything) does your endurance say about your character?* Communities and individuals are driven to seek meaning as endurance generates questions of worth and value. Spiritually, endurance and stamina can hinge upon what we think suffering means.

Belonging with suffering doesn't mean that you deserve what you suffer or that you are reconciled to it. It doesn't mean that you don't wish for suffering to cease. Belonging with suffering doesn't mean that you've got its meaning figured out as part of the big picture or some other personal narrative. It just means being open and vulnerable to transformation by suffering. You probably don't know how this suffering will transform your life, but you nevertheless accede to be transformed.

If belief in the afterlife gives meaning to your suffering, you can show endurance, stamina – and love – as a pilgrim and sojourner who only truly and completely belongs in heaven. If your view of suffering is more Buddhist, you realize that you're *already* in some relationship with suffering. Either way, endurance and stamina provide the time and energy to belong with suffering.

3. **When you idealize endurance and stamina for peak experience or excellence, you strive but fail to belong with suffering. Likewise, when you idealize love for romance or a good cause, you strive but fail to belong with suffering.**

A popular individualist and subjective version of these religious narratives is the quest for peak experience in physical endurance exploits. This is the hope and conviction that one will enjoy a "personal high" if only one endures long enough. Whether you view this inner reward as transcendent enlightenment or dopamine-intensive satisfaction, the capacities for endurance and stamina are introspective enough to make inner reward meaningful even for the rock climber who summons endurance and stamina to reach a very real and external summit. However, when suffering's meaning is reduced to a goal, one does not learn how to belong with suffering. Instead, suffering is shunted as quickly as possible from one location to another like a parcel in a bank teller's pneumatic tube.

Turn your gaze outwards and inner reward might be replaced by distant excellence. Again, suffering's meaning is reduced to a goal: attaining excellence, but no one learns to belong with suffering (least of all with failure). Besides, it's not even *real* excellence. This excellence is shiny, empty, and out of reach, but nevertheless puts strivers on probation as inadequate disappointments. This faux excellence intimidates without inspiring and looks like mediocrity's unimaginative *way of understanding* "excellence."

Real particular excellence of any kind makes distinctive concrete demands upon movement capacities such as endurance and stamina, in the context of other capaci-  ties. Specific particular excellence does more: it risks those capacities in a challenge to create and embody a new standard. Every instance of real excellence is a "game-changer." Witnessing actual instances of excellence can inspire and motivate you. Merely upholding and seeking something called "excellence" does not. Substitute "true love" for "excellence" and you get pretty much the same result.

If you're inclined to idealize endurance and stamina for the sake of inner reward or some standard of excellence, beware. Endurance and stamina are not ends in themselves. Philosophers of the body have criticized the tiresomely disembodied arguments of western philosophy which treat persons as incorporeal and genderless minds. Alternative fitness philosophies and practices have mushroomed in the past thirty years, in part, as reactions against what I would uncharitably describe as a bastard child of Western Philosophy: *the fitness gym.*

Upon one fitness gym machine, the Stairmaster,® the unengaged mind meets the dislocated and relocated body. Together they go nowhere, think about nothing, and deliberately belong nowhere, for the sake of an external excellence called "fitness." It's not existential absurdity, but how do you charitably and accurately describe this person and activity? No real climbing up stairs happens. "Exerciser" and "user" are impersonal terms for this sweaty earnest soul. This exerciser will never master these stairs while working hard to develop cardio-respiratory endurance and stamina. Happily, this goal is worthwhile, commendable, and reachable on the Stairmaster®. Unhappily, people tend to become the very thing they practice most intensely. And what exactly does one become from this practice at the top of topless and endless stairs?

4. **Because endurance and stamina demand meaning, as does love, the most serious problem for these capacities is neither exhaustion nor opposition, but disillusionment.**

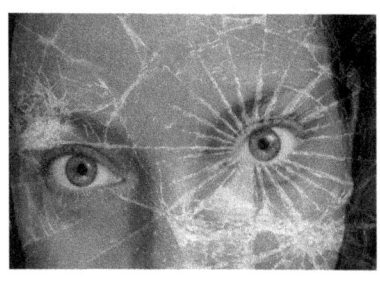

We should not leave our discussion of endurance and stamina and what these dogged capacities teach about love without considering their greatest enemy: disillusionment. How do you keep moving when your illusions are shattered? The trauma of disillusionment can last a lifetime. That's worse than the "agony of defeat," because failure is specific and concrete. Disillusionment steals meaning itself. In *Intimations of Immortality from Recollections of Early Childhood* (1802), William Wordsworth expresses it beautifully:

There was a time when meadow, grove, and stream,
The earth, and every common sight,
To me did seem
Apparelled in celestial light,
The glory and the freshness of a dream,
It is not now as it hath been of yore; -
Turn wheresoe'er I may,
By night or day,
The things which I have seen I now can see no more.

- William Wordsworth, *Intimations of Immortality from Recollections of Early Childhood* (1802)

One of the hardest things for an individual, community, or nation to endure is disillusionment, because illusion buoys activities. When it's gone, you feel betrayed even when no betrayer can be named. Unlike a belief, an illusion is not disconfirmed or refuted. You outgrow it or else it is shattered. Wordsworth provides a clue to why disillusionment is so hard to endure. He remembers and mourns a lost childhood illusion. He remembers what he "*now can see no more.*" Without illusion, meadow, grove and stream are just dirt, water, and weeds. The memory of the landscape remains, but the illusion is gone.

You may have discovered this yourself on some well-intentioned but ultimately disappointing sentimental journey. Clever digital technology may re-create the landscape, but the illusion which makes it memorable is impossible to restore. Like Wordsworth, we long for what we haven't forgotten but which we can't recapture. Our childhood illusions no longer belong to us. We may adapt by saying that we're better off without illusions, but we feel heavier, not lighter.

Outgrowing illusions is natural as our place in life changes. But shattering illusions is another matter. That's not just swapping an inadequate picture of the world for a better one. Someone vandalizes your inadequate picture. You no longer trust your relationship with the world. Emotionally, you feel lost. This is suffering endured with nowhere to belong. The illusion-buster may be right about your illusion being false and silly, justifying the shattering as "for your own good." [29] But the illusion was your raft on life's river. Remember the feeling of romantic infatuation? A certain girl or boy seemed perfect, but the raft sank. As you tread water, you can search for the lost infatuation in the hope of finding love, but you won't swim with endurance and stamina in any direction until suffering recovers meaning, until you belong with suffering rather than fleeing it. By "belonging," I don't mean stewing in despair but rather being intentionally open to transformation (and not just anger, shame, or despair). You'll then find more endurance and stamina than you believed possible.

I have dealt with love so far mainly in terms of interpersonal relationships, but you may think of love as an expanding circle which moves outward from friends and family to more distant or abstract commitments and cares. Disillusionment has much the same effect when a cause has been buoyed by illusions about its prospects, purity, or rightness.

Since we have treated belonging and transformation in the framework of animal capacities for movement, let your animality put love's illusions into perspective. In nature, predator and prey move in an ongoing interplay of illusions. Through camouflage and mimicry, animals fool each other about their location and intentions. This is as true for courtship as for predator and prey. Without illusions, animals would have nature's equivalent of "last call" in a dance bar when all the house lights are turned up. Not a pretty sight. The dancers need their illusions, and illusion may be the last dance keeping them together even as they strive to last until the bar closes in the hope of finding love. Hesitate before ridding someone of illusions unless you really do have something better to substitute. Love's illusions are neither incidental nor entirely optional. Likewise, they may enable us to belong with and endure suffering.

Albert Schweitzer's observation is appropriate here: *"The soul too has its clothing of which we must not deprive it, and no one has a right to say to another; 'Because we belong to each other as we do, I have a right to know all your thoughts.' Not even a mother may treat her child in that way."*[30] The answer to disillusionment is not to inoculate every striver and lover against illusion, but to recover, or help others to recover, the kind of directionality which dares to risk and belong with suffering, with or without illusions. That's love at its most formidable. That's love which endures.

PART THREE

LIVING WITHIN LIVES

CHAPTER 11
The Politics of Transformation

The 25 meditations in Chapter 2 began with my two-word benediction (you belong) and closed with the claim that *your life belongs in every other life, and every other life belongs in yours.* That introduces the "where" of your belonging, but we also need the "how" of political practice to handle conflict and make policy. Political transformation means being open to qualitative change or what we refer to as "real change." These would be not merely changes in the mechanics of governance, but changes in polity's quality of life. If you lament that nothing really changes in politics and that justice demands real change in how things work, what you seek is political transformation. That's not transformation of lives by politics but rather the polity's vulnerability to real changes.

My claim about all life belonging in yours, and your life belonging in all lives may sound like Eastern mysticism. You may think I'm claiming that borders between individuals are illusions because all life is interconnected and truly one. I am not making a claim about interconnections or ultimate oneness. No, whatever the truth may be about the oneness of life, belonging is not communion. Living within lives makes life sustainable, and perhaps meaningful. This is not about connections and relationships *between lives.* Whether you're a rugged or ragged individualist or the most communal of souls, I'm claiming that every life belongs in yours, and your life belongs in every other life. Certainly your right brain, left to its own devices, does not experience your life as a self-contained unit, and Buddhists may be right to pin enlightenment on that intuition. Every life (acknowledged or not) is already part of your life, and your life (welcome or not) belongs in every other life. It is up to us as to how we honor or dishonor that belonging in our interactions and relationships.

If your sense of belonging is more proprietary, this is a lot to swallow. You might have preferred instead to belong at a specific address, inside a familiar setting, with a true soul mate, or where you're meant to be. If you want belonging which begins with you and spreads out like concentric ripples, you won't find it here. I don't see how that kind of egocentric belonging can result in any political transformation. It is more intimate than belonging to a flag or a cause.

Put life's belonging in the widest possible context; animate organic life is situated in the inorganic and inanimate cosmos and draws matter and energy from the cosmos. All life is made of star-stuff, but life never really belonged in this cosmos. This misfit is much too fragile and the cosmos is too harsh. The only place where life belongs is within lives. You belong in *all* lives because you are vulnerable to every one of them. You are not equally attached to them and may know only a few, but none has borders excluding you. Though people pretend otherwise, no life can *make you* not belong. Life and belonging don't work that way. The vulnerability of belonging trumps places, borders, exclusion, and every claim to contingency. Before life strives, it belongs.

What do you make of this openness politically? If this stark vulnerability on all sides is what you want politics to fix, you do not want transformation. If every

The Politics of Transformation

life belongs in your life, your life might feel colonized or exceeding maximum occupancy. If your life belongs in every other life, you my feel spread very, very, thin. Does life belonging within lives make you feel paranoid, presumptuous, grandiose or intrusive? Your feelings indicate reliably what you actually believe about your life's borders. More to the point, you believe that your life *has* real borders. You're not used to thinking otherwise. Each organism separates itself from the abiotic world in some fashion. However a cell's membrane and your skin are not borders for life. That's just packaging.

To figure out belonging in political practice, I invite you to become a new abolitionist. Abolish non-belonging. That's why you need an ethos of transformation in which core values such as peace and justice arise from your own activities and capacities. Accept that you already belong in every life, and that each life belongs in yours. You're unshakably situated to confront a political status quo where belonging and meaningful activity are not taken seriously. What should we make of this status quo? In Chapter 4, *Please be Seated*, I called it protracted inactivity or doldrums. Kim Stanley Robinson's future-history in his novel *2312* describes our near future as the "great dithering.[31]"

The great dithering of ever-busy yet never-active politics plays conflict-generating games of belonging vs. non-belonging. But if everyone awakens to discover that they belong (and always did), that they live within other lives which likewise live in theirs, the games are over. Politics no longer merely manipulates people but risks finding itself transformed by real human needs, hopes, and values.

Until then, the great dithering makes any prospective political transformation appear so wildly idealistic and feel so supererogatory that no one could hope for transformation. You can only dither and despair that any meaningful change could ever escape that bottomless gravity well. Ironically, for all its inertia, the great dithering is surprisingly wobbly and paranoid from the inside out because its leaders have no secure sense of belonging (!) Their chickens have finally come home to roost.

Therefore, begin with conviction, confidence, and the humbling certainty that you do belong, always did, and always will. You therefore matter and may give or receive this blessing with any living being. Those many lives belong in yours just as yours belongs in those lives. Moreover, you all belong with authority requiring no further justification or legitimacy. Don't trust political authority which doesn't clearly belong in any lives and barricades itself against lives.

Within the ethos of transformation, power, as application of force to make a difference, is real enough, but it is ultimately only one capacity among our others, and power is never a sure bet. Because power gambles capacities such as strength, balance, coordination, and endurance, power has little to work with if these are lacking. Without effective power to make a difference, authority can only resort to more force. The problems of "power politics" are often really problems of "impotence politics."

As this politics presumes to keep trading belonging like a scarce futures commodity, does belonging have a chance in hell? The political stakes are high enough: so long as life's belonging remains a ball in play, life essentially belongs nowhere. The endgame of belonging nowhere is violence against life, human and non-human. I wish to argue that political transformation means practicing politics as *discipline*, which I discussed in Chapter 4, "Rethinking Discipline." Discipline is the praxis and engine of transformation. But it only makes sense if you accept life's belonging-saturated world. I want to argue for three claims, with emphasis upon social and political transformation:

1. **Because each life belongs in every other life, you need a politics of belonging before you have a trustworthy politics of borders. Otherwise, borders create violence and**

injustice instead of protecting vulnerability to change.

2. **Disciplined power as commitment to and capacity for qualitative change arises from belonging and allows political transformation. Disciplinary power fosters bias and conformity, makes belonging contingent upon compliance, and undermines political autonomy.**

3. **Practicing disciplined power does not eliminate bias and coercive uniformity but undermines their authority and autonomy. The authority of belonging and the autonomy of your capacities jointly subordinate bias and coercion to values of courage, justice, peace, truth, and love.**

A public commitment to acting as though all life belongs may sound politically radical, but no more so than the nightmare of great dithering. This belonging is not amnesty nor squatters' rights in which everything belongs "as is." Instead, landowners are not entitled to pretend that they don't fully belong in the public realm, and that the state cannot pretend that certain classes of people belong nowhere. This politics no longer makes belonging contingent upon necessary and sufficient conditions, or even good behavior. Belonging is thereby liberated from demands of citizenship, terms of membership, or any other status. Those who violate other's rights are accountable because they continue to belong in every life. Politics should cease making non-belonging criminal while institutionalizing non-belonging as punishment.

**

1. **Because each life belongs in every other life, you need a politics of belonging before you have a trustworthy politics of borders. Otherwise, borders create violence and injustice instead of protecting vulnerability to change.**

How do you go about abolishing non-belonging? The fascist solution is to eliminate everyone deemed to not belong. That abolishes people who don't belong, but the hotel of non-belonging remains standing, now with plenty of vacancies. It doesn't take long to find new occupants. We generate groups of non-belongers in abundance: homeless, disabled, refugees, illegal aliens, in transit or transitory, tourists, loiterers, part-time employees – the list goes on. Our animal capacity to sort our environment into categories of safety and danger, in and out, has an autonomy and momentum which no amount of reason, compassion, and experience can budge.

Elementary school teacher Jane Elliott memorably taught Ohio third-graders about the impulse to sort and discriminate in the 60's by getting them to pretend for several days that blue-eyed classmates are better than brown-eyed classmates, and then vice versa. A class which had belonged together congenially then fractured and turned on itself. Just after the assassination of Martin Luther King, Jr., Miss Elliott wanted to teach those white kids about discrimination and stereotypes. That's the educator's optimism: Learn control, forbearance, and restraint about your categories. Show yourselves more reflective, tolerant, and discerning than your old categories. Censor those offensive categories or else invent more inclusive categories.

I am not an optimist about eradicating bias or prospects for never-ending end-runs around bias. Sorting and bias are so hard-wired into how we make sense of the world that even the flimsiest and most arbitrary discrimination can feel plausible and meaningful. Justice, love, or truth nevertheless confront bias and conformity with a more compelling authority: belonging. Paradoxically, your vulnerability to transformation is your most authoritative strength for confronting bias. Unlike bias, belonging needs no self-justification, claims to legitimacy, or continuing reinforcement. Don't mistake the persistence of bias for autonomy or decisive authority. You may not be able to budge the badger out of its burrow, but you can corner it there. If justice is the flexible reach of strength against resistance, let bias serve as resistance.

The inclusive solution would be to erase all borders, open all doors, and turn away no one. If there are no outsiders, non-belonging has been abolished. Unfortunately, this would also abolish our clear expectations for each other. If we don't know what to do with each other, how do we belong? This inclusivity also smells like presumption, for opening the gates implies a self-appointed gatekeeper. Belonging need not be contingent upon open or closed gates.

Take belonging off the table, and a border becomes a line useful insofar as it represents clear and reasonable expectations. People belong where they live on different terms, symbolized by borders. But when the border means that certain people do not belong, borders create zones of non-belonging and make your belonging contingent upon where you live. The endgame of non-belonging is violence against life, so, if you belong only on these terms, you will hear news of violence in such zones as though it emerges senselessly from "nowhere." You can't fully identify with victims of such violence because you believe that no one belongs there or could ever belong there. In effect, you do not belong in their lives and those lives do not belong in yours. So, defending borders won't make everyone belong where they live. You can't make people belong.

When two groups try to make themselves belong by excluding each other, they equally lose a sense of their belonging. Exclusion feels like strength, but, unlike your actual strength (exercising force against resistance), exclusion feels increasingly restless, restricted, and scared. You don't experience more belonging by fortifying it with walls and contingencies. Exclusion as a corollary of membership only means not meeting certain expectations. You might not be a citizen. But your passport to belong remains. You still belong in every life, and every life (citizen or not) belongs in yours.

The habit of using borders not simply to represent our expectations for each other but to establish belonging makes people on both sides of the border feel lost.

Non-belonging and contingent belonging create the same sinking dread we feel when lost somewhere, unable to recapture a sense of security. Surroundings begin to look hostile and you feel disoriented and very much alone. The political irony is that this lousy state of affairs prevails on both sides of the border even as people blame those on the other side for their dread.

Take belonging off the table, and feeling lost is not such a crisis. You belong, even if you're not sure where you are. Don't worry about being in the middle of nowhere. Because every life belongs in yours just as yours belongs in every life, there never was a "nowhere." If you're still not sure of where you are, take heart. That is exactly what you experience during transformation, and, somehow, it's where you always belonged.

"You are the light of the world. A city on a hill cannot be hidden." – Matthew 5:14

Even a shining city on a hill must decide whether its borders are simply useful expectation markers or ways to establish people's belonging. Is this city fortified or open to everyone? Where does the city on the hill toss its trash? Do widows, orphans, lowlanders, and strangers belong here? Do dissidents and misfits belong inside the city's borders? We think of police and military as protecting borders and protecting lives. However, the police can't prevent people from shooting you. All the force in the world's arsenals can't protect you from war or defend species from extinction. And we don't really care about protecting a line on a map.

But we should protect belonging, for that's vulnerability to cherish. Peace and justice, put into action through balance, coordination, strength, and flexibility, are worth protecting, not as abstractions, but as ways in which we actively and specifically live together. Belonging is not about abandoning borders and citizenship. It's ceasing to make those contingencies arbiters of belonging. Politically, people can be invited to belong, admonished to belong, or reconciled in belonging. Political belonging is civic vulnerability to changes which matter. Call it keeping the peace or doing justice, but what's defended is our civic vulnerability to transformation. To that end, borders are enforced and preserve our expectations for each other. Biases about who belongs and who does not are hard to resist, so don't resist. Instead, be open to transformation. Don't let bias hold it hostage.

2. **Disciplined power as commitment to and capacity for qualitative change arises from belonging and allows political transformation. Disciplinary power fosters bias and**

conformity, makes belonging contingent upon compliance, and undermines political autonomy.

Think of borders in terms of discipline. In chapter 5, *Rethinking Discipline*, we considered discipline as commitment to and capacity for qualitative change which fosters belonging. I am not nitpicking to say that discipline fosters (promotes or encourages) belonging rather than creates or establishes belonging. Your belonging is already a fact of life – probably the most basic one. Discipline is your daily praxis which isolates you from your surroundings so that may belong in those surroundings anew. However, this is personal discipline. Is there a political discipline for belonging?

Most utopias offer some disciplinary social caste system of people assigned to tasks, functions, or status. However, political discipline makes "freedom of association" sound less like Boolean motion of molecules and more like how we really exercise the best of our animality. This is collective political discipline with power, speed, strength, flexibility, balance, coordination, accuracy, agility, endurance, and stamina. This is not discipline as just another border to separate belonging (those with jobs) from non-belonging (those who don't belong). Shadow economies and under-classes are corollaries of this approach. Think instead of disciplined activity which builds and sustains a society in which courage, justice, peace, truth, and love are how our activities function.

The practice and training for a personal discipline isolates you from your surroundings and options (in a sense), and, politically, discipline means social activities undertaken as though you belong in all lives and as though every life belongs in yours. That may sound too sticky or packed for isolation, but political discipline isolates you from attachment to place, loyalties, affiliations, and relationships, not to break these cherished bonds, but to ensure that you and your bonds have belonging.

Every activity can be undertaken as discipline, and that may provide the grace and context for a cause which transforms a society. Albert Schweitzer makes a wise point about this: *"Only a person who can find a value in every sort of activity and devote himself to each one with full consciousness of duty, has the inward right to take as his object some extraordinary activity instead of that which naturally falls to his lot."* [32] Discipline makes borders for activity which represent clear expectations appropriate to our capacities and faithful to our values.

You might think that we could avoid bias, discrimination, and non-belonging if we replace disciplinary compliance with impartial principles.  In *A Theory of Justice*, John Rawls' famously argued that the reconciliation of liberty and equality, and a fair and just distribution of primary social goods, requires distributors to don a figurative "veil of ignorance." They would decide how to distribute primary social goods by feigning ignorance of their own stakes and status in society. That's isolation in the sense of adopting an ahistorical "original position." Rawls encouraged us to think about the principles we would agree upon when ignorant of our own status and standing in society. *A Theory of Justice* provides an account and defense of those principles.

This neo-liberal approach to justice is also disciplinary inasmuch as it relies upon principles to enforce borders and compliance. In Chapter 7, I characterized justice as the flexible reach of strength against resistance. However, relying upon disciplinary principles alone to ensure justice would mean flexibility without strength. Behind the veil of ignorance, we may strive within the permissible scope of our principles to be fair, but no provision is made for strength to meet resistance.

Thorny problems of distribution and entitlement are generated and propped up by bias and demands for disciplinary compliance, but notice that those who suffer injustice are treated as a class apart. They presumably *do not belong* until distribution is rendered fair. Their belonging is made contingent upon justice. In the meantime, they must be content with belonging nowhere. The privileged who profit rather than suffer from injustice are assumed to have no problem whatsoever belonging. I invite you to question this picture. If privileged and oppressed lives all belong in your life, and your life belongs squarely in these lives, this may not even the score, but it does put the score in a new picture as lives now vulnerable to transformation by other lives.

3. **Practicing disciplined power does not eliminate bias and coercive uniformity but removes their authority and autonomy. The authority of belonging and the autonomy of your capacities jointly subordinate bias and coercion to values of courage, justice, peace, truth, and love.**

The difference between a strong athlete and a powerful one, or a strong performance and a powerful one is that, while strength applies force against resistance, power summons strength as well as other capacities to make a difference. If you wish you had the power to drown, bury, or otherwise eliminate bias and coercive uniformity, but despair that any of this ever really changes, remember the badger. You may be powerless to get it out of its burrow, but you can keep it there. Stubborn staying power is not authority. Life holds final authority and legitimacy because life belongs. Bias is a sorting trick with delusions of grandeur. The individual and collective exercise of power focuses and invests speed, strength, flexibility, *et al.,* and puts bias and coercive uniformity in its place.

In the United States, it is natural to think of the millions of undocumented immigrants as an issue for the politics of belonging. What do borders mean? If borders represent protection of those inside from outside intrusion, these millions do not belong. Non-belonging makes them prey to exploitation, violence, and injustice. The political fiction of non-belonging creates and justifies underclasses. If borders represent merely expectations with associated penalties and prerogatives, we have no stake in believing that some people belong and that others do not.

Undocumented people belong in the lives of every other person in the United States as neighbors, workers, and cultural presence. Each American belongs in their lives, not only in public services, but also education, employment, and other shared activities. Citizenship is put into a different perspective as a way of honoring belonging with specific expectations. Citizenship does not constitute or define belonging but instead presents the "how" and practice of belonging on specific terms. Think of belonging in these inter-situated ways, as lives belonging in lives (for where else could life belong?) rather than in places, and citizenship is not rendered meaningless or impossibly complex. It is simply one system of coercive conformity and compliance of the sort that Michel Foucault recognized as features of the modern age. Belonging is a much bigger and far more basic status for life than legal sanction.

Does disciplined power make borders permeable or semi-permeable? No. It subordinates bias and coercive compliance to values of courage, justice, peace, truth, and love. A society, whatever its borders, is alive and growing. It is not a museum full of artifacts to preserve. It is not a medical quarantine, and not a national park. Everything seems to belong in museums, except the visitors. They wander uncertainly or with faux seriousness, placeless or at least chair-less, from one exhibit to the next. I recently wandered around in Prague's Museum of Decorative

Arts. Among religious treasures and Hapsburg glassware, the museum displays intricate 17th century timepieces which were cutting-edge engineering and navigation science in their era.

Through the exhibit area's open window, I saw the Jewish cemetery with its medieval tombstones. Why had the Nazis left it untouched after obliterating many such cemeteries in Europe, as well as Prague's entire Josefov ghetto? I was chilled to read that Hitler intended it as an exhibit for a museum to an extinct race. Whether that story is true or not, the cemetery teaches a lesson about the politics of transformation. You belong by being open to qualitative change. Being prey to injury and violence is not readiness for transformation. Where then does Europe's looted Judaica belong? Wherever it will transform societies and polities. Each life belongs in every life, every life belongs in each life, and belonging means readiness for transformation.

If this no longer sounds like covering the world in flypaper and even makes some sense, what practices would this ethos abolish? What opportunity does it provide for resolving conflict? This ethos would expose political games predicated on contingent belonging as the shadow shows they always were. It would put the legal fiction of non-belonging on the defensive. This ethos opens a door to conflict resolution by summoning people out of their mutually exclusive turfs and into their already shared lives. That's good political housekeeping, if nothing else.

Conservatives should like this ethos for its accountability and focus on core values. Liberals would delight in its diversity and lack of oppressive marginalization. However, when conservatism buys preferential belonging by excluding everyone else, this ethos holds no appeal. If liberalism insists that belonging is about ever-wider inclusivity, this ethos would perplex them. If everyone already belongs, what's the point of trying to make them belong by widening your circle (or theirs)?

Non-belonging is a political fiction which everyone believes as a true story. Stop believing that story and you'll find no "outsiders" to keep outside or to bring inside. There never really was an inside or an outside to belonging. Whether it's underground economies, illegal aliens, under-classes, refugees, or prison inmates, that political fiction of inside/outside still packs a punch. It makes millions of people functionally invisible as if by political and economic stage magic. It's possible to pretend that they all belong nowhere only if you keep believing in nowhere.

In closing, I'm reminded of a comic's rhetorical question, *"What will all the preachers do when the devil is saved?"* If everyone belongs, will any life have a sense of belonging, or is human life stuck with inside/
outside ways of belonging expressed in bias and coercive conformity? Within Christianity, the universalist conviction that all will be redeemed and joined with God, has never been so popular as theologies which neatly separate the elect from the damned. To put the question a different way, how much patriotism could you really muster about being a world citizen?

On some level, we're aware of Bertrand Russell's paradox about the "set of all sets" when we think of belonging as a grand unity or whole greater than the sum of its parts. Russell asked whether that super-set would be a member of itself or not a member of itself. Either option leads to contradictions. Our ethos spares us that dilemma. Instead of claiming that everyone belongs or should belong to some super-set which neither belongs to itself nor to anything else, we simply observe that each life belongs in every life, and that every life belongs in each life. This would be a more workable way of being a world citizen

Disciplined power confronts disciplinary coercion most effectively when it does so with the authority of belonging. Individuals and groups can invest these capacities to make a difference which puts the idea of "nowhere" out of business. Violence seems pervasive, "senseless" or "coming out of nowhere" only when people's map of belonging pictures vast expanses non-belonging full of under-classes and shadow lives.

You may be waiting for this shoe to drop, so here it is. If every life belongs in yours, that includes plenty of people you never knew, don't like, and may fear and hate. Notwithstanding, they all belong securely in your life (and you're welcome!) Your precious life belongs in the middle of theirs, even if you hate the thought of belonging in such sordid lives. If this makes you squirm, take comfort in the realization that this inter-situated and inter-dwelling humanity, still in need of much reform, nevertheless now makes a little more sense. We might not be satisfied with reform. We might demand transformation.

CHAPTER 12
Virtual Belonging

Telepresence, low-latency telerobotics, and human spaceflight are leading to redefining what constitutes an "explorer." – Buzz Aldrin, *Mission to Mars* (2012)

Virtual belonging is an important but slippery and elusive way to belong. Online, you belong as a ghost! I've argued that kinesthetic intuitions about courage, justice, peace, truth, and love are experienced in the physical exercise of your capacities. I've also argued that, notwithstanding, these capacities

(power, speed, strength, flexibility, *et al.*) can be as much mental as physical; and as genuinely political as physiological. Power and endurance are not just about twitching muscles and heavy breathing. It's harder to say what these capacities mean when you introduce mediating technology. I've also argued that non-belonging is a fiction, but what does that mean in a culture of virtual belonging?

Mediating technology allows you to virtually belong with people or situations when you are absent. Consumer technology such as cell phones, smartphones, and computers do what telegraphs and telephones once did: they enable what Buzz Aldrin calls "telepresence;" you virtually belong to exercise influence when you're someplace else. The technology for that virtual belonging, whether old or new, typically keeps you sedentary and inactive. You remain seated (See chapter 4, *Please remain seated.*). I don't care whether technology makes you passive, or inactivity biases you to favor technology which allows you to remain seated. Either way, you remain seated.

Mind you, participating in simulations can be very active and demanding. One thinks of pilots in flight-test simulations. Simulations are engineered to summon responses and impose movement demands of prospective environments. That simulation may be good enough to feel and look just like the simulated environment. Normatively, you might even prefer the simulation as a hyper-reality so overwhelmingly and positively engaging that non-virtual environments seem pale and mundane. By then, the word "virtual" is virtually out of business, isn't it? We have two isomorphic but distinct domains for interaction. How do we know which is real? And must one be more real than the other?

However, I am less interested in skepticism or metaphysical judgment calls than what virtual belonging actually means for your basic belonging and transformation. Virtually belonging has become as familiar and mundane as making a phone call. But what does this mean for belonging? When I'm on the phone or online, I am situated without reference to place, but no one seems confused by this free-floating state of affairs. No crisis of belonging emerges, and yet we intuit that this is different than, perhaps less than, living within lives. The issue not the mediation of technology, but how we imagine ourselves together in the midst of mediation. I believe that Geoffrey Wong has an excellent alternative perspective on virtual interaction. He understands virtual reality in terms of our ability to be actors:

"Acting is not just a form of expression, but a fundamental way of knowing. To act is to become someone else, in another set of circumstances, and thereby

know and experience different reality. By giving his/ her body over to a character, an actor enters a character's reality and he can be said to embody (or provide a body for) the character. The character lives through the actor, but so does the actor live through the character. An actor in cyberspace is no different, except that the body he/she gives to her character is not his/hers; but rather his/her virtual one. He/she embodies the character but he/she, personally, is embodied by cyberspace. This is a very powerful metaphor, and greatly simplifies the problem of creating complex environments..." - Geoffrey Wong (1996)[33]

This makes sense for how you and I virtually belong. When communicating on the phone or online, you and I pretend (in some ways) to be in proximity. Therefore, being online or on the phone are not confusing ways to belong together. They are well-understood forms of role-playing. This is not acting in the sense of creating a theatrical illusion of my presence or yours. It's an agreed-upon acknowledgement of each other while playing a part. This works because our experience with non-virtual belonging presumably gives us intuitive confidence to balance access gained and context lost during virtual interaction. One challenge is not to overstate or misrepresent these gains and losses, but to put them into perspective as we navigate virtual belonging. I wish to argue for three claims:

You Always Belonged and You Always Will

1. Pretending that you belong is not a lesser or fake belonging. Virtual belonging has the potential to liberate belonging from dependence upon place and locale by letting us explore how each life belongs in every life, and every life belongs in each life.

2. Virtual belonging compromises the terms of life's belonging (vulnerability to transformation) when it supplants the non-virtual exercise of human capacities for power, speed, strength, et al.

3. Virtual belonging is embedded in a culture of protracted inactivity, but it has the potential to enrich a culture of meaningful activity and belonging. We have the power to write that story as we choose.

Rather than rushing to judgment about social media as "non-community theater," let's admit that it's hard to get our bearings online. Whether you dive in with gamer control fixations or dizzy disorientation and lack of perspective, borders give way to custom-made virtual terrain. For example, you know that social media gratifies a need for belonging only up to a point, and that interfacing electronically isn't the same thing as showing up. Being able to access millions of people online doesn't mean any one of them belongs in your life or that you belong in theirs. "Access" isn't even a social or relational term.

Notwithstanding, for the first time, those millions of lives are made manifest to you and you to them, in social media. Gossip threads aren't much of a beginning, and predatory hackers and snoopers give "each life belonging in every life" a sinister meaning, but that doesn't mean you can't give and receive the blessing that you belong even when you're absent.

**

1. **Pretending that you belong is not a lesser or fake belonging. Virtual belonging has the potential to liberate belonging from dependence upon place and locale by letting us explore how each life belongs in every life, and every life belongs in each life.**

The scope of virtual reality mediated by technology is much broader than we realize because so much of that terrain has become background of our lives. We typically think of computer-assisted interaction as the main platform for virtual reality, but people make low-tech or non-tech virtual realities when they collude to live in the past or the future, or they lose themselves in compelling stories. Financial systems can be massive virtual realities built of virtual assets. Belonging becomes a ball in play. Virtual reality happens in real vehicles too. We collectively pretend to be in private spaces as we drive on public roads. We pretend to be in private conversations while we talk publicly on cell phones.

I believe in the potential of virtual belonging to liberate and revive our sense of belonging, but I think we are in a time of transition which requires pretending, as Wong claims. We act "as if" we belong in situations from which we are absent. We have not yet developed the knack of virtually belonging in ways which might dispense with role-playing. I suggest that people most often pretend to be disembodied ghosts in virtual belonging. That role carries a strong appeal as old as Plato's story about invisibility ring of Gyges. In *The Republic*, Glauon tells Socrates the story of a shepherd (an ancestor of King Gyges) who unearthed an invisibility ring. Freed of any fear of punishment, Gyges steals, despoils, and kills. A ghost has no residency or sense of belonging, even at its favorite website. No courteous "goodbye" is expected when these ghosts depart an online community. They simply vanish.

Pretend to be a friendly ghost or a scary one, but ghosts float around with no stable location except where they choose to lurk and can do as they please without suffering consequences. There's something unsettling about that. Connection without commitment, input without sacrifice, access without intimacy, anonymity without responsibility, relationship without risk; a somewhat self-indulgent form of belonging, but then we're not accustomed to belonging in so many lives in the course of a day. You may feel the need to protect yourself from having too many lives belong in yours. It's bound to be awkward, and the ghost is a transitional fiction for us. We belong, but in a somewhat apparitional and non-substantial sense. Ghosts can visit but can't be pinned down.

I disagree with Wong that living beings can be meaningfully embodied by cyberspace, avatars notwithstanding. "Embodiment" is already such an oddly spiritualist or science fiction conceit. Minds, selves, souls, and persons do not pour themselves into or solidify into some organic epiphany called "embodying." People have shown that they pretend online in many different ways, and the format is typically that of a searching spirit.

For example, in Chapter 8, *Balance and Coordination: Matched Partners for Peace*, we considered the meaning of hospitality as articulated by Immanuel Kant. Hospitality is an ancient value which humanizes our place-loyalties by recognizing that we belong in each others' lives. Even with the best of intentions, it's presumptuous to extend hospitality if you have no space or place to share, but you can pretend to share ghostly space and place. You can make ghostly gestures like confirming "friends" on Facebook or offering access. If Wong is correct, we pretend to share cyberspace just like finite and discrete places on the earth's surface where we live, even if it's grudging accommodation in tight quarters.

However, ghosts don't have muscular capacities. For all their shape-shifting, they have no ethos for transformation. Do you show agility playing a video game or doing an online simulation? You need certain game skills, and they're satisfying, but, other than moving your fingers, you are physically inactive. You can't claim agility if you don't change your posture or direction. You can simulate shifting rapidly between environments and unexpected challenges to which you must respond rapidly. This tracks agility closely, but it's not agile movement because you don't commit your body to any rapid change in position or direction.

French teenager David Belle and his friends made up *parkour* or free-running in the 90's based on the obstacle course training of Belle's father. In French, an obstacle course is *un parcours de combattant*. Some play *parkour* games online. Players manipulate cartoon *traceurs* through a variety of

vaults, sprints, and landings. It's "parkour" (*l'art du deplacement*). It's French enough to be existential and to thumb its nose at organized sports. Parkour is the art of moving through environments as swiftly and effectively as possible using only the human body (not just your fingers). This gymnastic and practically acrobatic agility can be play or "jamming," done alone or with a group.

To see parkour *traceurs* jamming as they run, jump, and climb helps you to appreciate that slow horizontal movement is merely a conventional mode of belonging as you move. They traverse walls, roofs, and urban obstacles with grace, improvisation, and agility to show that "obstacle" is a relative term when people put their bodies (not their fingers) on the line or upon whatever ledge they can grip without falling. How should you describe someone proficient at ghostly online free-running or simulated rock-climbing? I'm sure the French have a word for it, and I doubt that it's "agile." While we should not underestimate the mind's ability to transfer skills from one context to another, it's unlikely that virtual belonging affords experience of our muscular capacities.

No matter how fast or powerful our technology, online busyness is not an experience of moving with speed and power. Despite it's apparitions, the ghost lacks substance. Online environments collectively have a pushy totalizing character. Digital realms increase size, connection, and access with categorical momentum. There is simply no way to push back as in other environments. You are only a pretend ghost, after all.

2. **Virtual belonging compromises the terms of life's belonging (vulnerability to transformation) when it supplants the non-virtual exercise of human capacities for power, speed, strength, et al.**

Whether you love being wired or loathe technologically mediated interaction, as more of your interactions become virtual, you become increasingly busy but proportionately less active. That means less intuition and confidence about those possibilities of movement which give courage, justice, peace, truth, and love kinesthetic credibility. You may still believe in those values, but you might not expect to experience them. In that sense, virtual belonging supplants the activities of life's basic belonging wherein we get a feel for those core values.

Moreover, as the sphere of virtual interaction expands with technological insistence and commercial ambition, how long will you credibly pretend to be embodied or to belong within that sphere? After all, you will experience belonging's proximity and constraints less and less frequently. At some point, you may forget how to pretend and worse still – even forget why you bothered pretending at all. Why pretend to belong with people in a domain where you can multi-task and take access whenever you want it?

The problem is not your diminished contact with others or your distance; the problem is rapidly increasing virtual interaction between people in which their humanity has only the very tightest crawl space. The "out of body" experience is no longer restricted to mystics and near-death survivors, because it's an online norm, and we haven't found the best ways to humanize this expansive belonging. Emoticons won't do the job.

Meanwhile, as virtual belonging gradually supplants basic belonging, virtual belonging distracts people from such belonging. You recognize these complaints: *Move! You're blocking the TV! Don't interrupt me – I'm on the phone! Don't you ever check your phone messages, voice mail, E-mail, tweets, or online social networks?* While under the spell of virtual belonging, they act not simply preoccupied (e.g. reading a good novel), but as though they no longer belong where they live and, by the way, neither do you. *Can't you see that I'm busy?*

This is not a lament about social and psychological dysfunctions observed in children who spend a great deal of time interacting with virtual realities. That kind of lament was launched against television for 60 years with no victory because it missed the point. People sense that virtual domains undermine something basic about belonging, but they resisted only by moralizing and claiming that these domains make children do bad things. So, media critics harped on violence, junk advertising, or pornography. Social media critics often use this ploy. They *don't* mention the real point: what's happening to the child's confidence and certainty about belonging in the world and with others. I think that's far more important.

Although virtual belonging places lives within lives in new ways, its technology is increasingly portable and pervasive. It allows you to carry around play-acting instead of shared experiences of the world. Virtual realities are venues where we *pretend to live and belong,* more comfortably and usually with a greater sense of control than we do in our actual surroundings. That's operant conditioning to which humans are not exempt, and such effective positive reinforcement is hard to resist (if resistance is what's needed.)

I am enthusiastic enough about the possibilities of virtual belonging for improving (but not transforming) lives that I don't want to overstate risks or launch into a jeremiad. However, on the phone, online, or in our cars, we can remain sheltered in virtual realities without experiencing the joy of belonging that comes with exercising their capacities for movement. This is not Garrett Hardin's "tragedy of the commons[34]" in which public spaces are left barren due to lack of personal stakes, but a "tragedy of the silos." Tightly wired but disconnected; wholly accessible but cocooned inside info-shells. What began as role-playing for virtual belonging can turn into tailor-made operational solipsism.

For an otherwise mobile, intelligent, exploratory and socially interactive species with over 700 muscles making up half ones body weight, our stationary and sedentary fixation on virtual belonging, if it is not robustly humanized, can be isolating. Instead of being ready and vulnerable to transformation, you would protect yourself from such change. We already live with one consequence of this inactive inward-turning: a numbed non-respect and casual disregard for others in our vicinity. When people talk on cell phones as though bystanders don't exist or matter, that's only a recent version of your defensive uncaring which casually turns any animal trying to belong where you drive into road kill.

This may strike you as alarmist. I hope that it is. Virtual belonging has provided ways for people to belong anew with others, but if we no longer want to be vulnerable to transformation, then we allow, by default, relational vacuums in the places where we actually live. That gives new space and place to abuse and violence. To live as though ones place and the place of others need not be taken seriously, can foster a belief that virtual belonging (belonging nowhere or anywhere) matters more than belonging some place in particular. If it matters more than your belonging, do you still matter? How many snubs add up to an assault?

3. Virtual belonging is embedded in a culture of protracted inactivity, but it has the

potential to enrich a culture of meaningful activity and belonging. We have the power to write that story as we choose.

So, what would make belonging in real places more compelling than pretending within simulations and virtual belonging? Here's one philosophical argument, courtesy of Samuel Clemens (a.k.a. Mark Twain): *"The difference between fiction and nonfiction is that fiction must be absolutely believable."* Nonfiction is under no constraints to be believable or imaginable, yet that is where life experiences belonging. We wrongly associate the incredible, unexpected, novel, senseless, or bizarre exclusively with fiction and make-believe. Belonging in real places can be more surprising and compelling than virtual domains because, within our animal capacities, we experience our humanity.

Enchantment with new abilities in virtual belonging can make the non-fiction world seem only a flat and static status quo. This reminds me of the C.S. Lewis' story, *The Silver Chair*, from his *Chronicles of Narnia* series. In the story, Prince Rillian is trapped in a silver chair each night by the Green Lady, presumably because he has psychotic dreams and would change into a serpent if released. In fact, the Prince is sane and healthy at night and struggles then to escape the enchantment that nothing is or can be real outside the Green Lady's cave. That is the silver chair's spell. The Prince struggles to believe in meaningful activity and deeper belonging while under a spell of non-belonging and remaining seated.

In Chapter 1, I provided some stories from my life to illustrate the dynamics of belonging, so I'll make up a story here. This is a story about the Virtual Amphibians.

The Virtual Amphibians

Once upon a time, fish dreamt of evolving into amphibians and pretended to escape the water by acting as much as possible like the amphibians they dreamed of becoming. They simulated what they thought walking around would feel like, and the pretending became popular entertainment and social recreation as more fish joined in. Endless variations on amphibian make-believe pervaded this fish culture. In fact, it all but supplanted fish culture. The fish paid less attention to their actual schools in which they swam or to their surroundings. They immersed themselves (so to speak) in virtually leaping out of the water, whenever they got the chance. As virtual amphibians, their lives now acquired entertaining adventure without danger, control without responsibility or risk of failure, and connection to other fish without having to really pay much attention to them.

Some fish moralized that pretending to be amphibians was an incredible waste of time and bordered on delusion. The other fish responded defensively that it was only fun and harmless make-believe. It was also preparing them for a new wave in their species' bright future. They began to forget how to be fish or to care much about being fish. They were especially annoyed with fish who showed up, didn't pretend, and would not swim away. As the bubble for virtual amphibians grew, fish no longer knew how to swim with a school but, as virtual amphibians, they could instead move in amazing new ways in domains they never imagined.

How would you finish the story? Does the virtual bubble burst? Does life continue swimmingly? Do fish simply choose whether to act like fish or amphibians? Or does the bubble simply keep growing as more life and care are devoted to it? The closest philosophical cousin to this bubble is the *monadology* of philosopher Gottfried Leibnitz (1646-1716). Many critics (and quite a few thinkers interested in virtual belonging) have pointed to Leibnitz' uncanny foresight. He conceived of indefinitely many substances individually programmed to act in a pre-established harmony. These substances never really interact, and, within the monadology, there is no need to distinguish between inside and outside. What you think of as "outside" is just an inside being unpacked and revealed with greater clarity.[35]

Our fish in the bubble are somewhat like Leibnitz' real and exact metaphysical points, but not real fish. Monads are the impenetrable plenum of an infinitely dense universe but are without extension of their own (welcome to the Internet). That's not a bad metaphysics for virtual belonging. It feels like the best of all possible worlds because everything already fits together even as it grows and reveals new levels of complexity without the trouble of connections. Monads are never transformed and are blessed with inertia. They never really belong not even within the plenum, but they are no less awesome for that. Perhaps they will get their wish and evolve into amphibians.

It may sound as though I have attached a string of dire caveats to virtual belonging. I neither urge futile resistance to virtual belonging nor endorse its the expanding domain. We are still writing its story as its sphere expands with no end in sight. Leibnitz' description of the monadology is worth remembering:

'Everywhere and at all time, everything is the same as here'.

So where do you belong?

CHAPTER 13
To Boldly Belong

Again, suppose that *you belong, therefore you matter.* Is that still true if you happen to be an elk? How about a beaver? I can't think of any reason why it wouldn't be.
Beavers' lives are routinely transformed by what they encounter. As for transforming environments, beavers are our fellow engineers. Like *homo sapiens*, no beaver is content with an environment "as is." Again, suppose that *each life belongs in every life, and every life belongs in each life.* This claim is even more true for the biology of the beaver-generated wetlands than for human interpersonal relationships. Although we act as though an impassible standing forest separates human values from those of non-human nature, the

all-gnawing beaver makes short work of standing objections. So, when you think about whether human beings can belong in nature, you don't need a different philosophy of belonging and transformation.

We've considered how our animal capacities combine to provide our kinesthetic experience of courage, justice, peace, truth, and love. If you care about how human beings belong in nature, these animal capacities for movement have special meaning because humans learned the meaning of power, speed, strength, *et al.* from observing how other animals move; some animals likewise became our icons for courage, justice, peace, truth, and love. That is no coincidence. As I argued in Chapter 3, *Animal Crackers*, accept this as confirmation of what you normatively experience in your own muscles. But are you willing to take the next step and entertain the possibility that non-human animals likewise experience "human" values, albeit on different levels and on different terms? Nature "red in tooth and claw" unsurprisingly belongs with us in a shared ethos of transformation. I invite you to consider these four claims:

1. **Relationship differs from belonging because relationship means interaction between distinct lives. Belonging means living within lives.**

2. **Belonging is not "one right way," "one right place," or a perfect relationship with nature. It is vulnerability to transformation. Belonging includes dislocation, relocation, conflict, tension, and risk. Belonging is a fact to live with, not a goal to strive towards.**

3. **Human lives belong in nature's life no less than nature's lives belong in ours. We should act accordingly.**

4. **Human beings can also belong in nature far from Earth.**

**

1. **Relationship differs from belonging because relationship means interaction between distinct lives. Belonging means living within lives.**

If we affirm e*ach life belongs in every life, and every life belongs in each life*, what counts as "each life" in nature? We've taken it to mean a solitary human being. However, life belongs not only as solitary selves, but also communally as groups, teams, orchestras, swarms, and biomes. Life is open to transformation on many levels. It's hard to individualize certain species such as the royal jellyfish which is a virtual spaceship of individual polyps. Life belongs whether viewed as honeybee or swarm, but we should not conflate the meaning of *relationship* with the meaning of *belonging.* We are too quick to do this when speaking of a whole and its parts.

To describe life as a part of a greater whole, or as a whole subsuming constituent parts describes a specific relationship, but not necessarily vulnerability to real change. This is worth considering soberly and carefully because we casually speak of membership and inclusion as ways to belong. The problem is that *relationship* is not about how life belongs in many lives or how many lives belong in one; relationship is about terms of engagement between distinct lives.

Both relationship and belonging can be meaningful, but they are different. A relationship is a matter of degree ranging from nominal and superficial to deep and abiding. Belonging is not a matter of degree. It is openness to transformation. You can contrast being in a relationship to being outside a relationship or in no relationship. However, if non-belonging is a fiction, life has no place "outside belonging" or not belonging at all. You may work at your relationship, but you don't have to work at belonging.

Because of our personal investment in relationships, it may sound wrong-headed to separate belonging from relationship. But consider: when you define belonging as the sum of ones relationships, you imply that life is pitiably incapable of belonging outside those relationships. But you belong. You always did, you always will, and you matter. As a matter of practical reason, don't go looking for belonging in relationship. Bring your belonging to that worthwhile and meaningful relationship and honor the belonging you find there. If that relationship is less than optimal, belonging might open possibilities.

If we look at life with the widest possible lens, is that where we find belonging? In the 1970's, physicist James Lovelock and microbiologist Lynn Margulis, proposed the Gaia Hypothesis, now referred to as "Gaia Theory," (GT). GT claims that the Earth's living biosphere has been closely integrated throughout the planet's history with the Earth's thin membrane of atmosphere, cryosphere, hydrosphere, and lithosphere. Together, life and the Earth's surface shaped by life comprise a complex interacting system – a super-organism - which maintains the climatic and biogeochemical conditions on Earth necessary, and perhaps favorable or even optimal, to sustain life. In other words, life makes and keeps the earth a place of belonging for life.[36]

To Boldly Belong

Whether this shaping of Earth's thin habitat membrane over eons is providential, evolutionary, or a remarkable byproduct of living, it's clear that life's belonging - diverse vulnerabilities to transformation – has co-existed with life's vulnerabilities to death and extinction. However, we run into Russell's "set of all sets" paradox if we appeal to Gaia to confirm that life truly belongs on Earth. Does Gaia belong to itself or not? Neither answer avoids contradictions. If Gaia belongs to itself (whatever that means), then it cannot be transformed by anything else. Its constituent species may evolve, but Gaia itself would merely change without being transformed. If Gaia does not belong to itself, but instead belongs to Earth, its belonging is hostage to Earth's fate. Before you speak of spaceship Earth and Earth as Gaia's lifeboat, think carefully about that metaphor. Lifeboats imply rescue and the hope of reaching shore. There is no rescue and no shore. Gaia is onboard the Flying Dutchman sailing forever.

Speaking of life on this global scale and across eons as a super-organism does not demonstrate belonging, but it does give a different meaning to life and death. For super-organism Gaia, no life and no species is a "keeper." Human beings might still feel on the outside of this immense belonging and striving, and moralize about why they deserve no better. But, if each life belongs in every life, and every life belongs in each life, then *each life is born and dies within every life. Every life is born and dies within your life.* Did you suppose that your own birth and death are contained only within your life? Did you forget all the births and deaths packed within your life? These questions invite you to think about celebrating births and grieving death with new meaning.

2. **Belonging is not "one right way," "one right place," or a perfect relationship with nature. It is vulnerability to transformation. Belonging includes dislocation, relocation, conflict, tension, and risk. Belonging is a fact to live with, not a goal to strive towards.**

Let's begin with a story about a mollusk. Imagine a clam, snail, octopus, or giant squid. We've allowed muscular vertebrates to hog the stage too long. How does a mollusk belong in nature? Sand allows a mollusk to quickly bury itself in the surf. Carried along by water currents, the mollusk winds up elsewhere, but it belongs no less for being buried or transported. This mollusk belongs in every other life. I am not assuming a vast intricate network of macro-connections and micro-interactions with every creature great and small, though marine biology reveals plenty of that. I mean that this mollusk belongs not just within invertebrate taxonomy or inside a specific habitat but as a featured or bit player within every other life.

Exactly how this mollusk belongs may be apparent in a marine environment or dazzling in a pearl necklace, but I claim more: that it belongs even in lives utterly distant from and without any apparent *relationship* to that mollusk. Its belonging is not about the sum of its relationships. This mollusk makes no discernable difference to most life. Notwithstanding, *no life excludes the mollusk from belonging in its life.* The mollusk may do nothing with that belonging bequest. If it had a soul, it might believe belonging is reserved for more social animals. Nevertheless, this single transitory mollusk is inter-situated with every life. And all lives belong within its life, regardless of its shell size.

And they all belong in yours, regardless of whether you think your life amounts to very much. You may object that, without relationship, belonging is only metaphysical cotton candy without substance or stake. To the contrary, you belong when ready and liable to real change, and that can mean suffering, tension, conflict, and risk.

Sometimes we tease apart *relationship* from *belonging* by making relationship the means to ultimate belonging as our goal. One risk of this means-end tactic is that one relationship or set of relationships is expected to produce belonging. This is unfair to belonging because treating it as a goal makes belonging a future target rather than an abiding fact of life. In effect, it means acting as though you do *not* belong (yet). It's also unfair to your meaningful relationships because you have saddled them with a job. Relationships deserve to be valued or reformed on their own terms.

Another risk of making relationship a means to belonging is that you may try to belong in nature only by some ideal and sustainable relationship. This relationship would presumably make human presence in nature seamless, spontaneous, non-problematic, effortless, and easy. And sustainability presumably means never having to say "good-bye." One popular version claims that some tribe figured out this "right way" long ago but we have since sadly and conveniently forgotten that relationship. Before 1492, Amerindians tried many different ways of belonging in the Americas: Sioux-nomadic, Cherokee-agricultural, Aztec-militaristic or Tlingit place-bound to the arctic. They worked in different ways, and their belonging produced very different landscapes and consequences for nature. Why should we expect one ideal right answer to the question of how humans can belong in nature in the 21st century?

Perhaps you're optimistic about belonging in nature. You have a deep spiritual sense of place in nature, and you aspire to do no harm to nature. You grow your own food and cherish the land. This is commendable, and I do think that you belong with every other life in an ethos of transformation - but how are you ready to be changed by all the non-human lives which you cherish? How will those lives belong in yours apart from gaining your favor and your forbearance?

Perhaps you're a pessimist. You think it's too late to belong in what's left of the nature we've ravaged. What humans call "protecting nature" is really a protection racket by which we extort assets from nature. Where's belonging amidst extinctions and accelerating pointless destruction of habitat inflicted by humans? Nature is a carcass we've gutted, and "belonging in nature" is a self-indulgent conceit for affluent and privileged people with lots of security to fall back on. Moral outrage makes more sense than any pious talk of belonging.

All the same, injustice is fought best when victims, helpers, and offenders know that they belong and therefore matter. If all belong, all are accountable for acting accordingly. Exercising our strength within the scope of our values is how we answer injustice. We act against resistance within the reach of our values and principles. Nature exercising its strength against resistance within the reach of its improvisations makes a similar answer to injustice. You belong in lives treated unjustly when you are vulnerable to their hardship, and that's one of the few graces of climate change. Although some bear the costs more than others, there is no inside vs. outside. We all belong.

3. Human lives belong in nature's life no less than nature's lives belong in ours. We should act accordingly.

This is an environmental ethos, but not an environmental ethics (yet). This book's belonging has been descriptive but not prescriptive except within my occasional manifestos. What kind of "should" emerges from this ethos? Do we have principles, rights, or binding obligations about belonging in nature? What clear moral direction do these inter-situated lives provide? How ought we to act accordingly? If "ought implies can," we could be in trouble because "act accordingly" doesn't spell out what we can mandate, prohibit, or permit. Even with good intentions, means, and opportunity, what counts as unethical for belonging in nature?

Recall that "you belong, therefore you matter" is not one claim entailed by another. It is a claim affirmed and invoked by a benediction. That you should act accordingly doesn't just imply that you can; it actively extracts that "can" from your descriptive possibilities through invocation and commitment. Ask the question negatively: How would you act as if you do not belong in any life other than your own, and as though no life belongs in yours? How would you act as if you believed that you neither belong nor matter? *Circumspice!* – and then do something different and better.

If all life (including dangerous life) belongs in yours, how do you act accordingly? This is nature's version of hard corollary that all human lives (dangerous or otherwise) belong in your life. *First*, do not conclude that, because you hate or reject that life, it does not belong in your life. *Secondly*, do not conclude that, because you refuse to identify with these dangerous lives, you do not belong in them. You do.

Belonging is not about good relationships and is not a relationship at all. Belonging is an inter-situated fact of life. If you reject that fact, danger and violence (human or nonhuman) are experienced as outside threatening to force their way inside. Danger and violence seem to belong nowhere yet spring from elsewhere. We find ourselves under the illusion that danger and violence are inexplicable invasions from a land of non-belonging.

Accept belonging as a fact of life, and that life belongs in lives, and you find danger and violence in the middle of your days, just as you belong in dangerous and violent lives. That increases the odds that you will respond appropriately. It decreases the odds that you will first resort to violence, not because you thereby identity with violence and danger, but because it was never really elsewhere. Our ethos doesn't protect us from danger nor require us to prohibit violence, but it cuts danger and violence down to size. As you belong in nature, you are open to transformation, but you remain vulnerable to loss. Suffering loss can both traumatize and transform lives.

Acting accordingly means not pretending that life does not yet belong or that its belonging is contingent, or that this belonging "hangs in the balance" or languishes in some probationary limbo. Acting accordingly (or acting at all) means faith in your

capacities for meaningful activity, despite a culture of protracted inactivity.

Gaia theory states that all living things on earth are interconnected so as to create one organic whole. This whole is a self-regulating system which is commendably constructive, intriguingly goal-directed, and dauntingly complex. You can divide this super-organic whole into parts (yet another classic stage trick), once you decide what sort of division gives you meaningful parts. It may depend on what you're researching. Ironically, James Lovelock first tested the premise of the Gaia hypothesis as a researcher for the Jet Propulsion Laboratory, investigating the possibility of life on Mars. He reasoned that, if such life existed, it would have transformed or altered the Martian atmosphere to accommodate itself. No such transformation was apparent.

4. Human beings can also belong in nature far from Earth.

Suppose a skeptic asks: *"Do human beings really belong on Mars?"* How do you answer? What do you think it means to *belong* someplace?

Do you agree with the skeptic that only standing on Earth can summon any real emotional attachment and sense of belonging? If so, you agree with the skeptic that Mars is a harsh environment where no life belongs. You may be sure that humans can endure Mars, confident that humans can conquer its challenges, and be committed to a permanent human presence on Mars but, unless you also believe that people truly belong on Mars, long-term settlement is out of the question. People won't prolong their stay someplace without a sense of belonging. A sense of belonging emotionally tethered to Earth can only hold its breath until it's back on Earth. To explore and settle Mars, we need not only engineering and political will, but also credible confidence that people can belong on Mars.

Human beings can be very creative at turning unfamiliar and inhospitable situations into places of belonging, but this ability needs to be cultivated and supported. That human capacity is just as important as coping with contingencies and enduring stress. Wherever they go, people need to belong where they live. They want to not merely survive and thrive, *but rightly so.*

When I say, "You belong," I speak to someone who's alive and not merely subject to change like a rock or a physical system but also vulnerable to *transformation*. That's a dynamic process with duration and direction, but, unlike change, transformation is life's distinctive way of risky and irreversible alteration. It's my hunch that life is so successful in transforming even the most recalcitrant external and internal environments because life itself has a knack for being transformed. I think that's true not only for life on Earth, but also for any past, present, and future life on Mars.

Do you want to belong on Mars? Very well, what kind of vulnerability can you bring? What transformations of understanding, emotion, perspective, and identity are you ready for? Before you judge your vulnerability as weakness, consider that it might be part of a new belonging. Before you worry that some vulnerability will undermine your sense of belonging, consider that it might unfold belonging. If you were as invulnerable to transformation as Superman or ageless as Peter Pan, you would also have as many belonging issues as Superman and Peter Pan. And how would you ever belong on Mars?

Those of us enchanted by the red planet have already been transformed in our imaginations, sense of the future, projects, priorities, and passions. If you persist in thinking of belonging as a *status* which someone declares, bestows, denies, or authorizes, then you're waiting for permission to belong on Mars. If you persist in treating belonging as attachment, bonding, sentimental clinging, or ecological at-onement with Earth's biosphere, you hold belonging hostage to a place in the rearview mirror. Instead, consider your capacity for qualitative change. Vulnerability in this sense is not necessarily a weakness. Understandably, those planning manned deep space missions do their engineering and psychological best to minimize human vulnerability, so mission architecture has a belonging blind spot. Correct this by bringing belonging fully into your field of view.

Belonging is life's gift to cosmos, transforming time and space into narratives and places. Belonging is how we experience not just being alive, but being alive and *rightly so*. Our primary responsibility to others, young and old, is transforming environments into unfolding places of belonging. Of course, you can't make yourself belong. You can't make others belong. But you can share and honor that belonging which is already transforming your life by contributing new possibilities of belonging on Mars. Life doesn't just sustain itself; life enables life to belong, whether on Earth or on Mars. It's a mistake to think of "belonging on Mars" in terms of how we might transform Mars. Think instead of how Mars has already transformed you.

To Boldly Belong

What's the sweet ratio between belonging and striving on Mars? My bet is that belonging, whether on Earth or on Mars, should always slightly exceed striving, even though striving takes the risks needed to open new possibilities for belonging. When striving gets too far ahead of belonging, striving loses meaning, and risks becoming absurd. You do not want to be 35 million km from home and find yourself in existential crisis, asking, *"What the hell am I doing here?"*

Belonging is not just about being inside a habitat or any other place where you think you belong. Belonging is vulnerability to those qualitative changes which legitimize and sustain your striving. Instead of asking where we might find life, ask where life belongs. Life has always been a fragile albeit stubborn misfit in a harsh cosmos. It never really belonged. So, life took care of that by belonging within lives. Those who figure out how to belong on Mars will already belong within the lives of millions of people on Earth.

Our society can commit to an ethos of creating conditions for belonging, even if we have to go to Mars to do it. But you can't make anyone belong on Mars. Even with the best technology, you can't even make yourself belong on Mars. That's not how belonging works. One of the ways we belong is that long-haul vulnerability which we call endurance, but that's not as important as readiness to become something completely new and different and to belong within lives which now yearn to belong within yours as you walk on Mars. That's why you belong in nature on Earth and on Mars.

You belong, therefore you matter. Don't make your value hang upon being human, being unique, being rational, most favored by God, or being the repository of some intrinsic value. Belonging makes life matter, and you already belong. That's enough authority to respect and cherish. You may think nature has only taught you that striving makes life possible, but, in the midst of that striving, extend this benediction "you belong" to nature which already blesses you. Striving does make life possible, just as belonging makes life matter. There's a reason that the lock seems to fit your key. Welcome home.

CHAPTER 14
25 Epigrams

I've offered a framework for thinking of life in terms of transformation both through striving (transforming internal and external environments) and belonging (vulnerability to transformation). For vertebrate animals with muscles, these transformations are combined and mixed in characteristic capacities for activity. I suggest that animals combine these capacities in proportions which human beings experience and label as values: courage, justice, peace, truth, and love.

A politics of transformation is possible when politics no longer treats belonging as contingent. Even virtual belonging is possible, giving us new experience of life within lives. Virtual belonging doesn't yet contribute much to our experience of values, but that may change with technology. Humans can belong in nature *not* by ceasing to transform the world around them, but by becoming transformed by that living world.

You may wonder about the moral and ethical implications of these claims. Is there any binding duty to belong where you live? True, there is a "must." The terms of belonging may be negotiable and normative, but the fact of you belonging as a life within lives is not. We call the stance and posture of detachment or alienation "non-belonging" but that's only a frame of mind. You're under no moral obligation to belong where you happen to live. However, if you insist on pretending that you don't belong because of your attitude and judgment (or that of others), you're wrong. At best, it's silly. At worst, it's morally negligent. The terms of belonging are dynamic, but the existential fact of belonging is not. If you're alive, you're squarely within lives (and they're well within your life). Work it out.

Does anyone have a right to be transformed? That would be a peculiar entitlement, but it does have meaning. If an institution or discipline promises to transform lives and fails, it has broken a promise. It might change you, but no transformation happens and is unlikely to occur unless you are ready to be transformed and this institution or discipline can facilitate new terms for your belonging.

So much of conventional ethics pretends, directly or indirectly, that each life belongs only within itself. Like Dither Duck, you and I assume that we belong only within our feathers. That makes the un-feathered world appear as an empty expanse of non-belonging. No wonder it looks cold and cruel! Building an ethics of relationship and interconnections on the shaky assumption that each of us only "really" belongs inside his or her own skin makes ethical practice hard. Ethics and politics are difficult enough without playing games of winning and losing belonging. I began our journey with 25 meditations, so I'll leave you 25 epigrams to ponder as you think about how belonging is honored or how transformation works in your life.

1. Before you judge values of courage, justice, peace, truth, or love, find out first what they feel like.

2. Transformation is not necessarily momentous, discontinuous, or miraculous. But it is irreversible. Transformation does not guarantee a wonderful outcome, but it's where we belong.

3. You can classify and measure change, positive or negative. Try to classify or measure

transformation, and you come up empty. Transformation is how life works at timely junctures, which makes transformation as improvisational, diverse, irreversible, and varied as life.

4. A life which transforms little and resists transformation is vulnerable to all the evils that come with living *as though you and others do not belong*.

5. Being excluded hurts like hell, so we expect belonging to feel like heaven. Belonging matters, but it's not heaven. It's not even an emotion. This insults our sense of symmetry.

6. Transformation is neither supererogatory nor superhuman. It's sensible and everyday without ever being humdrum.

7. Belonging is not probationary, problematic, scarce, or restricted to the lucky and few. It's simply living within lives.

8. Act with courage, and you find that justice, peace, truth, and love join in.

9. Belonging is not precarious. On the other hand, living as though you and others don't belong is

such a precarious and tottering conceit that it requires entire legal and religious systems to sustain it.

10. "Extremophiles" are organisms which can belong in inhospitable and unpromising circumstances. Let's extend this franchise and declare every organism an extremophile. That includes you.

11. People can change themselves or each other. But they can't make themselves or anyone else belong. Why did no one explain that to you when you were thirteen?

12. Twelve-step programs are said to work by giving addicts a sense of belonging in support groups. It's even truer that these groups enable addicts to believe that transformation is possible.

13. Believing that you can neither transform the world nor be transformed doesn't make you evil, but it might mean that you're not quite ready yet to be good.

14. If it sounds unbelievable that life belongs within lives, where else did you expect life to be situated?

15. Our society's numbing expanse of inactivity makes the prospect of belonging and meaningful activity seem larger than life - certainly bigger than *your* life. But belonging and meaningful activity are both exactly life-sized. You're a perfect fit.

16. Transformation is living in a right direction without seeing a destination.

17. If your recipe for change is plenty of strength and endurance, you might hold the world on your shoulders, but what do you strive and hope for?

18. If your life belongs in every life, and every life belongs in yours, then every birth and death is part of your life. Your birth and death are part of every other life.

19. Working out the terms of belonging is probably our most human activity.

20. Organisms and lives have insides and outsides, but that's just a life's packaging, not its scope, depth, and meaning. Each life is a bigger proposition than its wrapping.

21. Borders mark our expectations for belonging. They don't make anyone belong.

22. You're an animal, so you don't need a reason (even a good one) to move.

23. Are you not sure whether courage, justice, peace, truth, and love are real? You have all the capacities you need to experience them first-hand.

24. We're all vulnerable to change but less vulnerable to transformation.

25. You always belonged, and you always will.

Welcome home.

Bibliography

**

Abram, David. *The Spell of the Sensuous.* New York: First Vintage Books, 1996.

Capra, Frioff and Steindle-Rast, David. *Belonging to the Universe by* Fritoff Capra and David Steindl-Rast. San Francisco: Harper, 1993.

Casey, Edward S. *Getting Back into Place.* Bloomington: Indiana University Press, 2009.

Descartes, René *Discourse on Method and Meditations on First* Philosophy (Hackett, 2011)

Glassman, Greg. *What is Fitness?* Crossfit Journal, October 2002.

Heim, Michael. *The Metaphysics of Virtual Reality.* New York: Oxford University Press, USA, 1994.

hooks, bell. *Belonging – A Culture of Place*. New York: Routledge, 2009

Lewis, C.S. *The Silver Chair*. New York: Macmillan, 1953.

Lovelock, James. *Gaia – A New Look at Life on Earth*. New York: Oxford, 1979.

___. *The Revenge of Gaia: Earth's Climate Crisis and the Fate of* Gaia. New York: Basic Books, 2006.

___. *The Vanishing Face of Gaia: A Final Warning*. New York: Basic Books, 2010.[37]

Plumbwood, Val 'Belonging, Naming, and Decolonisation' in *Habitus: A Sense of Place*, Edited by Jean Hiller and Emma Rooksby. Ashgate Publishing, Ltd., 2005.

Robinson, Kim Stanley. *2312*. New York: Orbit Books (2012)

Russell, L.D. *Godspeed: Racing is my Religion*. London: Bloomsbury Academic, 2009.

Schweitzer, Albert. *The Light Within Us*. Escondido: Philosophical Library, 1959.

Taylor, Jill B. *My Stroke of Insight: A Brain Scientist's Personal Journey.* New York: Penguin, 2006.

Wong, Geoffrey. *The Philosophy of Virtual Reality. www.doc.ic.ac.uk/~nd/surprise_96/journal/.../ article1.html*

Endnotes

[1] An expert and compelling narrative of an eight-year recovery from a massive hemorrhagic stroke can be found in Dr. Jill B. Taylor's "My Stroke of Insight: A Brain Scientist's Personal Journey" (Penguin, 2006). My trauma was comparatively minor, but I recognize the emotional landscape of protracted and uncertain recovery she describes. Part of recovery is deciding and insisting upon new terms of belonging.

[2] The allegory of the cave, set forth in Book VII of Plato's dialogue, *The Republic*, is Socrates' account of the unenlightened human condition. Like a prisoner chained forever in a cave who can see only shadows cast on the back wall, we imagine that we know a great deal until we break free, discover that what we've seen are only shadows, and then climb to the surface to discover the world and the sun as source of life. The escapee then decides to return below to tell his companions. They do not believe him and attack him.

3   René Descartes, *Meditations on First Philosophy,* Meditation VI

4   "The ten domains of fitness" is a framework popularized by Greg Glassman, founder of Crossfit, Inc., and by Jim Crawley and Bruce Evans of Dynamax. Glassman describes these ten "domains" in his article, *What Is Fitness?*, Crossfit Journal, October 2002. This article is available at http://crossfitimpulse.com/wp-content/uploads/2010/04/CFJ-trial.pdf Dynamax presents these ten physical skills at www.medicineballs.com. Because these fitness programs promote general (rather than sport-specific) fitness, their regimens and workouts strive to incorporate all ten physical skills. I consider these physical skills as an anchoring dimension of broader and deeper capacities, the exercise of which allow us to experience core values and not simply vertebrate muscular movement.

5   Erin Manning *Relationscapes: Movement, Art, Philosophy* (2012), p. 13.

6   Steven Robbins, M.D. *"How footwear caused humans to become sedentary"* Invited lecture presented at KAHPERD International Sport Science Congress (ISCC) Daegu, Korea.

⁶ http://www.michel-foucault.com/concepts/ This site provides a brief but accurate overview of Foucault's view of discipline.

⁸ As we have discussed, postmodernist philosopher Michel Foucault interpreted discipline as a matter of politics and power in which the docile body paradoxically increases its personal power while being simultaneously subjected to the discipline, thereby losing political power and force. I am concerned here with the dynamics of belonging rather than power. When the goal for discipline is belonging, rather than power, disciplines developed through practice and training enable one to belong in the world in new ways. I do not mean to beg the question of whether power or belonging matter more for understanding discipline. I claim here only that discipline cannot be reduced to considerations of power without misrepresenting the meaning of discipline. In fact, power, in the strict sense of applying maximal force in minimal time, is itself a discipline developed through practice and training. Foucault elaborates his paradox of discipline in terms of power in *Discipline and Punish: the Birth of the Prison* (1977).

⁹ When I speak of discipline setting apart or separating the individual or community from its surrounding

concerns and circumstances, I do not mean this in the experiential sense of detachment, alienation, disinterest, or indifference. It is not a diminishing or dismissal of relationship but rather a beginning and strengthening of new relationships.

[10] Sec. 27. 'Though the earth, and all inferior creatures, be common to all men, yet every man has a property in his own person: this nobody has any right to but himself. The labour of his body and the work of his hands, we may say, are properly his. Whatsoever then he removes out of the state that nature hath provided, and left it in, he hath mixed his labour with, and joined to it something that is his own, and thereby makes it his property. It being by him removed from the common state nature hath placed it in, it hath by this labour something annexed to it, that excludes the common right of other men: for this labour being the unquestionable property of the labourer, no man but he can have a right to what that is once joined to, at least where there is enough, and as good, left in common for others.'

[11] The famous New Testament passage (Luke 12:48) is a longstanding cultural injunction binding great assets (strength) to commensurate obligation: *"but he that knew not, and did things worthy of stripes, shall*

be beaten with few stripes. And to whomsoever much is given, of him shall much be required: and to whom they commit much, of him will they ask the more."

[12] I am indebted to my colleague, John Sullivan, for suggesting the idea of a "pre-duty" which comes before and transcends other duties as a proto-obligation.

[13] A pre-duty could be called a sense of obligation which is existential and felt as binding, having to do with the human condition rather than specific relationships and entitlements.

[13] Pranis, Kay. *The Little Book of Circle Processes: A New/Old Approach to Peacemaking.* Intercourse, PA: Good Books, 2005. See also Pranis, Kay; Stuart, Barry; and Wedge, Mark. Peacemaking Circles: From Crime to Community. Living Justice Press, 2003.

[14] See *Doing Democracy in Circles: Engaging Communities in Public Planning.* by Jennifer Hall, Wayne Caldwell, and Kay Pranis. (Living Justice Press, 2010).

[15] A philosophically reflective and athletically relentless exploration of how rivers bring place and belonging together around water in living environments is

Akiko Busch's *Nine Ways to Cross a River: Midstream Reflections on Swimming and Getting There From Here*, op. cit.

[16] I'm indebted to Barbara Montero for bringing this chestnut to my attention and for her exploration of movement in her essay *Does Bodily Awareness Interfere with Highly Skilled Movement?"* Inquiry, Vol. 53, No. 2, 102-122 (April 2010)

[17] *Getting Back Into Place*, 2nd Ed., by Edward S. Casey (Indiana University Press, 2009), xii

[18] Thomas Seeley's *Honeybee Democracy* provides an excellent discussion of this issue, as does Jürgen Tautz' *The Buzz about Bees: Biology of a Superorganism* (Springer, 2009).

[19] Aristotle, *Ethics* II.9

[20] In this regard, the work of postmodernist philosopher Michel Foucault, and particularly his work *Discipline and Punish: the Birth of the Prison* (Vintage books, 1977) is pertinent. Foucault interpreted discipline as essentially as a matter of politics and power in which the docile body paradoxically increases its personal power while being simultaneously subjected to the discipline, thereby losing political power

and force. On Foucault's view, discipline is a dynamic of imposition and subjections. In contrast to this theory of discipline imposed on self or others, I characterize discipline as *intentional practice or training to make or restore places for life*. This is discipline conceived as a relationship between intentional activity and the world, not between subject and object (the body).

[21] As Foucault's theory of punishment and discipline illustrates, people find it hard to think about discipline as practice and training outside the framework of power, control, and subjection. Think instead of discipline as transformative activity which aims not for control, but for belonging. Perhaps belonging-discipline is the right kind of fire to fight Panopticon's wildfire of control-discipline.

[22] The story of Trinity Wall Street (St. Paul's Chapel) or "The Little Chapel That Stood" is worth investigating in detail. This quote is from the church's website: http://www.trinitywallstreet.org/congregation/spc/about.

[23] An excellent philosophical reflection and spiritual meditation and on this theme is *Gratefulness, the Heart of Prayer: An Approach to Life in Fullness* by Brother David Steindl-Rast (Paulist Press, 1984).

What do you think? Steindl-Rast argues that gratitude is primarily a relationship between gift and recipient (*being grateful for*). You can be thankful for some blessing in nature or life before you know who to thank, or even if you don't think there is anyone to thank. Of course, gratitude can also be a relationship between recipient and giver (*being grateful to*) but that's forced and insincere if you're not first truly grateful *for* some blessing or gift. He describes belonging as a gift which makes us feel gratitude. Is he right?

[24] The modern experience of alienation and estrangement are explored in modern philosophy, particularly the writings of Hegel, Marx, and existentialists such as Kierkegaard and Jean-Paul Sartre. Whether this separation between self in the world is a temporary wall of our own construction, or an enduring barrier not of our choosing, the wall can be viewed as hopeless, metaphysically necessary, a cultural crisis, or a personal dilemma. You may have endured enough angst and alienation to conclude that the wall doesn't come tumbling down whenever you want. You need a viable alternative to alienation. For now, consider that, although alienation is a compelling experience, it does not have the last word about our possible relationship with the world. There is also belonging. Begin by practicing agility and see where that takes you.

[25] *Belonging to the Universe:* Harper-Collins. 1992. (page 57)

[26] Ibid.

[27] When people act as though no one belongs, nothing is allowed to be mysterious. People only have substitute "away" domains of non-belonging. Mystery is dumbed-down to mean something opaque, inaccessible, or inconsequential. Mysteries become curiosities to entertain us in puzzles and stories. When people experience actual belonging, they encounter not only life, but its actual mystery. Mystics may have difficulty articulating and conveying such experiences. However, if you manage to experience, if only briefly, that your life belongs in every life and that every life belongs in yours, this is mystic experience. It's no less real and no less credible for that.

[28] When someone unilaterally inflicts figurative medicinal suffering "for your own good," get away. Unless you're targeted for a pleasant surprise, a concrete good (relieving your suffering) or participation in some greater good (the welfare of children), one-way unsolicited gestures are unlikely to be ethical, and you're likely to get hurt.

[29] *The Light Within Us* by Albert Schweitzer (Philosophical Library, 1959), p. 18.

[30] Robinson refers to a fictional future historian, Charlotte Stanback, whose periodization system labels the period from 2005 to 2060 as *The Dithering*. *"These were wasted years."*

[31] *The Light Within Us*, by Albert Schweitzer (Philosophical Library, 1959), p. 23.

[32] *The Philosophy of Virtual Belonging* by Geoffrey Wong *www.doc.ic.ac.uk/~nd/surprise_96/journal/.../article1.html*

[33] See "The Tragedy of the Commons," Garrett Hardin, Science, 162(1968):1243-1248. This famous article is reprinted in many sources, and is available in the new "commons" of online resources.

[34] A number of thinkers have commented upon the relevance of Leibniz' monadology to virtual reality and online presence. Michael Heim's text, *The Metaphysics of Virtual Reality* New York: Oxford University Press, USA, 1994 contains an excellent discussion of this relationship.

[35] *Gaia – A New Look at Life on Earth* (1979) presents Lovelock's hypothesis of Earth functioning as a super-organism or control system. His more recent books, *The Revenge of Gaia: Earth's Climate Crisis*

and the Fate of Humanity (2006) and *The Vanishing Face of Gaia: A Final Warning (2010)* take a darker view of how this control system, under a regime of global warming, may sustain itself at the expense of humanity.

www.ingramcontent.com/pod-product-compliance
Lightning Source LLC
Chambersburg PA
CBHW062044080426
42734CB00012B/2560